THE
COMPLETE IDIOT'S GUIDE® TO

Dating
for *Teens*

by Susan Rabens

ALPHA

A member of Penguin Group (USA) Inc.

Copyright © 2001 by Susan Rabens

International Standard Book Number: 978-0-02-863999-4
Library of Congress Catalog Card Number: Available upon request.

09   08   07   8   7   6

Interpretation of the printing code: The rightmost number of the first series of numbers is the year of the book's printing; the rightmost number of the second series of numbers is the number of the book's printing. For example, a printing code of 01-1 shows that the first printing occurred in 2001.

Printed in the United States of America

Publisher
Marie Butler-Knight

Product Manager
Phil Kitchel

Managing Editor
Jennifer Chisholm

Senior Acquisitions Editor
Randy Ladenheim-Gil

Development Editor
Suzanne LeVert

Senior Production Editor
Christy Wagner

Copy Editor
Catherine Schwenk

Illustrator
Jody Schaeffer

Cover Designer
Dan Armstrong

Book Designer
Gary Adair

Indexer
Brad Herriman

Layout/Proofreading
Darin Crone
John Etchison

Contents at a Glance

Contents

Introduction

"Dating!" What does this word mean to you? Does it remind you how uncomfortable it is to ask someone out or does it remind you of the fun you have getting to know someone new? Are you confused about how to get through the often awkward beginnings of relationships, or are you more concerned about how to survive breaking up?

I wrote this book as I remembered my experiences and those of friends, family, and clients. All of us remember the sweaty palms we got while reaching for the telephone, the anxiety about how to behave, and the intensity of a new relationship. But dating does not have to be a struggle. Like every worthwhile activity, dating involves certain tasks to learn and practice, and if you take the time to do so, you'll soon get better at the whole deal. Indeed, practicing the dating game will surely help you in your adult life of relationships. This book will give you some idiot-proof ways to allow you to be at ease and confident about dating. In considering dating today, I have included a number of tips, cautions, anecdotes, and stories.

A basic principle of this book is that dating serves a major learning purpose. Dating is the way people explore relationships. "Dating well" occurs when you learn to understand both yourself and the person you're dating. Dating allows you to learn what makes you and another person happy, satisfied, and excited; and success in dating gives you insight into what relationships are all about. Dating is one of the most fun learning experiences you can have, and it will develop in you a real sense of maturity, which you can bring forward into the next phase of your life. Enjoy these teenage years—and learn from them the ultimate lesson of good dating: Dating is relating, and relating is fun.

How to Use This Book

I think of dating as similar to the adventure and excitement of sports. Indeed, the activity has often been called the "dating game." Like any game, there is a setting or playing field, the actual play itself, some basic elements of training, and advanced techniques. The four parts of the book reflect each of these factors.

In **Part 1, "The Playing Field,"** I'll explore the environment of dating. You'll see what the nature of teen life is today and learn about the universal nature and fundamental principles of dating. I'll then zero in on the goal of this dating game—the development of relationships. With the field now prepared, you're ready to play.

In **Part 2, "The Dating Game,"** we'll embark on the real action. You'll learn how to ask someone out, and what to do when someone else does the asking. I'll discuss the different types of dates, some ways of keeping the game moving along, and the evolution of a dating relationship into something more serious. I conclude by a consideration of breakups and moving to the sidelines for a bit.

In **Part 3, "Training for the Dating Game: Your Behavior Is You,"** I shall investigate the elements of human—and in particular, teenage—behavior. As you gain some knowledge of yourself and the people you date, it's helpful to learn a little bit about emotions and motivations in general. I'll look at such issues as identity, values, emotions, decision-making, and parental influence.

In **Part 4, "Advanced Plays: Love and Sex,"** I'll explore what happens when dating becomes more serious. I'll consider physical intimacy—a complicated and absorbing issue if there ever was one—with frankness and honesty. These are inevitable issues in many dating relationships, and this book would be incomplete without discussing them.

It is my hope that by the end of this book, you will have gained a greater perspective of what dating is all about, and a greater appreciation for what the game can give you. The rewards of dating are many, both in general enjoyment and in lessons learned. And in the end, you will have gained greater discovery of who that person is who looks back at you from the mirror each morning.

Extras

In addition to the text of the chapters, you'll see many pieces of "extra" information in sidebars scattered throughout the chapters. I have grouped these into four distinct types, each with a sports-game theme:

Time Out

In these sidebars, I'll give you some tips on staying on top of your game on the dating field.

Penalty Flag

Here I'll help you avoid situations that could result in a penalty should you make some errors as you play the dating game.

Record Book

Look here for interesting statistics or informational tidbits to make the game more interesting.

Instant Replay

Here are anecdotes, examples, and case studies of real teens' experiences.

Acknowledgments

I wish to thank many people who have been of immeasurable help in writing this book. First of all, I wish to thank my husband, Richard Rabens, the best date I ever had and whom I continue to date and learn from. I acknowledge my own teenage sons, Daniel, Andrew, and Alexander, who have helped me understand teen life. To their many wonderful friends, I also extend my thanks for allowing me to share their experiences.

My psychotherapy colleagues have been a source of rich dialogue. My close friends have been ever-supportive of my efforts. And my clients—their parents and their children—have helped to educate me over the last 30 years.

In a book about teens and their families, I simply must pay tribute to my own parents, Victor and Louise Rosenblum, and my in-laws, David and Bertha Rabens, who cherished the delights of family life. My many siblings and my brothers-in-law and sisters-in-law still continue to teach me much about the dynamics of family interaction. My many nephews and nieces provide a constant laboratory for watching the joys of growing up.

I wish to acknowledge and thank my literary agent, Andree Abecassis; development editor, Suzanne LeVert; and acquisitions editor, Randy Ladenheim-Gil, for their encouragement and professionalism. Thanks are due to Christy Wagner, senior production editor, and Cate Schwenk, copy editor, for their editorial assistance. I am indebted to the entire staff at Alpha Books/Macmillan USA, Inc., for their work.

Trademarks

Part 1

The Playing Field

After much thought, Ben, 16, decided it was time for him to plunge into the dating game. He knew that many of his peers were already dating, and he wanted to know what he could ex-pect. He wondered, however, if this was what he should be doing, or whether he needed to have some special qualifications to date. How serious is it to ask someone out? What would dating imply about him?

In this part, I'll show you the "playing field," the setting of the dating game. I'll talk about the fundamental principles of the game and delve into the foundation of dating—which is "relat-ing." The building of relationships is what dating really is all about.

Chapter 1

The Teen Scene

In This Chapter

✧ The ways dating has changed

✧ Teen society today

✧ The modern elements that influence dating and relationships

Ben is 16 and is both excited and horrified that the junior prom is coming up. He knows someone he wants to go with but is very unsure how to go about asking her out. Does she even like him? What if she says "no"? How does he decide where to go after the dance? Will he seem "smooth" or just appear as awkward to her as he seems now? Will he ever be able to date with ease and comfort?

The difficulties Ben faces are probably familiar to you. They are common to all teens when they first start to date—and that's been true since the beginning of time. In this chapter, I begin by talking about some common challenges faced by teens, and then we explore how to meet them. This is about the playing field of dating—the teen scene of this day. Let's start by seeing where you and your generation are!

How Life Has Changed and How It Has Not

Let's say you live at the turn of the last century. You start to become attracted to another teen; something interests you about that person—their looks, smile, personality, something. You may not even know what attracts you—you just want to find out more about that person and you want that person to find out more about you. So what do you do? Do you ask them out to share a meal alone with you? Nope!

Dating three generations ago was a very different thing than it is today. In most societies, a young woman was never allowed to be outside alone, much less be with a boy without adult supervision. Getting to know someone was a very slow process that involved parents and chaperones, and there wasn't very much private time. At that time, even in some parts of American society, fathers selected grooms for their daughters, and couples barely dated at all before they were married. Can you imagine getting married to someone with whom you never went out?

The past century has flown by. And now, as we enter the new century, dating without chaperones has become a standard of the teen scene. While the rules of the game have changed, some of the same questions, jitters, and worries that your great-grandparents certainly had remain today for every teen trying to play this game:

- ✧ How do you ask this person out?
- ✧ What if this person says "no"?
- ✧ What do I do to get to know this person better?
- ✧ How can I tell this person about myself?
- ✧ Will this person like me?

Your great-grandparents didn't quite think about dropping over to someone's house to listen to CDs in their bedroom, but I guarantee you that they—as did your grandparents and your parents—had some of these same thoughts and concerns that you have today. We always see ourselves so differently from those who are older than us, and sometimes we can hardly imagine that our parents were ever teenagers. But, while members of each generation face distinct challenges growing up, they also share some of the same emotions and struggles as their ancestors did when they were the same age. I guarantee you that your parents had some butterflies in their stomachs before many of their dates!

Today's Teen Scene

Take a look at your generation. Believe it or not, you're part of a pretty powerful contingent (though it may not seem like it when you're trying to borrow the car). You and your peers support a huge amount of business. As a group, you have money—and spend a lot of it on clothes, music, food, concert tickets, and books. What you want to see on TV and in the movies determines much of what goes on the screen!

There's no doubt about it: You are a major force in this country and across the planet in terms of your numbers, economic power, and trend-setting. Industries supply your wants and needs, agencies address your risks and concerns, and the media follows you around wherever you go. American youth set the style for fellow teens around the world.

In fact, the teen scene begins earlier than the official thirteenth birthday. Younger pre-teen brothers and sisters in middle school (or junior high, as it is called in some places) are taking more and more of their cues from high school students. And although sixth graders may not be dating the way their older counterparts are, it is right around the corner for some. In fact, many pre-teens are deep into relationships. A 12-year-old told me that he was "dating" and even "going steady"—but to him and his peers that only meant eating lunch at school every day with one special girl. For this "couple"—and for their social group—it was a date for all the same reasons older teens go on a date. They talked and got to know each other.

The Free Society

Look at how open life seems to be today! If you watch TV, use computers, read magazines, and go to movies, you can see the whole world. How about MTV alone? At the very least, you see a whole range of ways people interact with one another, as well as different images of dating and being to-gether. The media gives you several examples of both the adult and teen world.

Conversation can be free-flowing as well. It seems like you can talk about anything at all—sex, drugs, money, religion— you name it. You are actually able to talk to friends and family about questions, experiences, and problems. Don't be misled, however, into thinking that there are no limits. Teens are still considered minors and legally do not have the same freedoms and rights as adults have. We may live in an open society, but minors are minors and parents are still in control in many areas.

School Daze

School is where you, as a teenager, experience much of your social life—in the classroom, through extracurricular activi-ties, or on the athletic field. And your friendships in school continue in your after-school world as well. You meet people in school, want to know them better, and begin to spend time with them after school as well.

School is like a small town, though. People love to swap sto-ries and gossip. Let's face it—we enjoy talking about relation-ships and who is dating whom. The gossip columns in any magazine or newspaper are among the most popular of reads! When one guy starts to hang out with one special girl, every-one likes to talk about it.

Penalty Flag

Don't forget that the person you date on Saturday night will be the same person you will have to face in school on Monday morning. No doubt your friends will talk about you and your new companion, so be prepared!

Future Shock

Although you'll continue to date into your adulthood, dating also helps you become more adult. One of your tasks during these teen years is to look at your adult years. Sound strange? Actually, most of you have already begun thinking about what you want to be and how you are going to get there. Your first step in the future is to decide what you'll do after high school. Will you go to trade school, get a job, or attend college? Maybe you'll take some time off. An important way to prepare for the future is to look at the present and to understand where you are and who you are. Think about what may be a cool career and a satisfying life, and then think about whether this is a good fit with you, your interests, your talents, and your ambitions. This time gives you the opportunity to explore yourself and how you will take your place in the independent adult world.

Friends to the End

One of the things you probably enjoy most is making and keeping friends. Some of you seem to do it more easily, and for others of you it takes some effort. You might think that people regard you as a nerd because you seem shy going up to a stranger or someone you do not know well, introducing yourself, and making conversation. But know this: Everyone experiences some hesitation at times. Remember that the people you want to befriend most likely want to be befriended! Everyone likes to get to know new people.

Time Out

Take advantage of the opportunities that dating affords. Being able to share your dreams and desires and discuss your future with someone you like and respect is a wonderful aspect of dating. Doing so will allow you to learn about someone else while you learn about yourself as you formulate your future personal goals.

You have heard the expression: "Make new friends but keep the old." Old friends are comfortable. You have a level of familiarity with old friends; you can often be apart from an old friend for a long time, but when you get back together it seems as if you just resume where you last left off. Sometimes it takes some work to keep these old friendships going. You may need to take the initiative to keep in touch and talk. But these are rewarding relationships to have—people who grow together with you and understand what you have experienced. We will discuss the role of friends and friendship more fully in Chapter 3, "Your Relationship with Relationships."

Having a large group of friends may make you feel included and involved, but you can't neglect your own individuality. Of course you want to discover how you fit into a crowd—or several crowds. But, you also need to figure out how you are unique. Going along with the crowd may be the easiest thing to do, but going it alone is very necessary at times. Your interests, personality, hopes, and dreams may not be totally in sync with those of all your friends. There are times to choose the activities in which you join your friends, and times to do your own thing.

Time Out

Think about dating as a way of actually building a friendship with another person. While there may be an element of romance involved, a fundamental of the dating game is getting to be friends with another person and allowing that friendship to grow.

Indeed, don't think that because you may want to go your separate way in certain areas and choose not to go along with the crowd means that you are unfriendly. Everyone needs some time alone to do things they particularly enjoy or to just get to know themself. Being alone is not the same thing as feeling alone or being lonely.

Modern Times

The teen scene today includes four specific new and recurring elements you need to consider. The automobile, a symbol of freedom if there ever was one, is probably a big factor in your life. So is money. Teens are now an economic entity unto themselves; they earn money and spend even more of it. The family, while always a part of a teenager's experience, has changed; as more and more parents work, the traditional "nuclear" family has been re-defined. And the technological

advances in the last decades have led to unprecedented approaches to communication and interaction. Let's examine
these elements one by one.

The Car

If you're like most of your peers, you're anxiously awaiting
the day you can finally get your driver's license. Getting a
license is a significant milestone for most teens. It means
freedom, maturity, accomplishment, and, of course, responsibility.

It is said that Americans have love affairs with their cars, and
teens are no exception. You are usually great drivers: Your reflexes are quick, and, because you've recently studied driver
safety, you know the rules of the road. But you do lack experience, which you can only receive through time and practice. Being with another person in a car adds another
element. Either you have the responsibility of being the
driver and safely carrying that person around, or you have
the responsibility of being the passenger and assuring that
you are safe. Good judgment is key.

Money Makes the World Go 'Round

Teens like to spend a lot of money on a variety of things,
which means they need a lot of money. You may have
money because you work for it or because your parents provide you with an allowance. Some of you have an allowance
from your parents for which you need to provide a service
in return, such as taking out the trash. Some of you need to
work during your free hours in the afternoons, evenings,
or weekends. Earning money by doing things in return is
how all of us make a living and support ourselves as well
as others.

Fortunately, it's easier than ever for most teens to find a job.
Some fast-food places and stores pay quite well for your labor
because they can't find anyone else to do the work. Teens in
the United States are involved in regular and summer work
in record numbers these days. While it may not be your

dream job, it is a taste of the work life to come—and a way to earn some cash.

Record Book

According to Teen Research Unlimited, teens spent $153 billion in 1999 alone, up from $141 billion in 1998. Girls spend $91 per week and boys are close to that, spending $87 per week. That is a lot of money that teens pump into the economy.

The Family Circle

A significant part of your life still revolves around your family. There are your parents and siblings—or other members—with whom you live and spend a large part of your time. As with your friends, you have relationships with family that, at times, can be a bit rocky. Parents and others may have different expectations of you than you have. And parents usually have rules.

Rules are often linked to values that your parents have and hold. They probably want you to adopt them as well. Some of these values are based on religious teachings; some on what they were taught by their parents; and some on your parents' own trials and errors. They have probably gotten into some close calls themselves!

Hi, Tech!

Technology plays a part in all aspects of our lives. Look at how you, as teens, take advantage of the tech revolution just in communication: You meet online, talk online, argue online, and make up online. Some adults have even proposed marriage online: How about the Internet as a matchmaker? Teenage Research Unlimited in 1999 reported in a survey that teens spend five hours per week actually dating, eight hours per week hanging out with friends, six hours talking on the phone, and four hours online. Kaiser Family Foundation in 1999 cited that 45 percent of all teens have Internet access at home.

Communication by e-mail is very much a part of the scene. Just be aware that this is a written record, so be sure that the write stuff is the right stuff.

Time Out

Keep the lines of communication open with your parents, especially when it comes to finding out about their values. Only by doing so will you be able to understand the rules they set and the expectations they have for you. You may not always agree with their conclusions, but it is good to know what their thinking is about.

Sex and Love

Sex and love are not necessarily the same! Your body is going through a lot of changes, and you are growing into a young person who feels comfortable with sexuality as a part of who you are. But this is somewhat difficult at times. Your physical appearance is transforming almost before your eyes. In addition, you sometimes have these emotional changes which you don't always understand—all of which are a normal part of puberty.

Penalty Flag

Never write anything in an e-mail you wouldn't want the world to read. E-mail is actually not much different from writing letters, except that it can be in real-time. Just be aware that you are committing your feelings and promises in writing. Be careful what you say in print!

Teens can begin to care about each other in a loving and nurturing way. The teen scene includes getting to know someone to see if the feelings of love begin to blossom. Love and sex often go together, but they don't have to. This is an important topic and I will discuss more about it in Chapter 19, "Ready or Not?"

Teen Dating in the New Millennium

The style of dating now has changed. Your grandparents may have been encouraged to date a single person for a long period of time (this was called "courtship"), while your parents may have dated many different people for brief periods at a time. They may have "gone steady" with a number of different people.

Nowadays there are many different dating styles, which we discuss in more depth in Chapter 6:

- ✧ One on one, in a pair
- ✧ Several pairs together
- ✧ Several people, unpaired
- ✧ In a group, some paired
- ✧ In a group, none paired

13

Record Book

In 1957, sociologist E. E. LeMasters looked at dating patterns of the 1950s, when many of your parents and grandparents were teens. He found that seventh and eighth graders were involved in group dates, ninth and tenth graders had random dating between "steadies," and eleventh and twelfth graders experienced steady dating. College-age folks were getting "pinned" (giving a pin as a token of going steady) and engaged, and women 19 to 21 and men 20 to 24 were getting married.

The configurations may be varied, but all are part of the dating game. All these variations have in common the desire of a single person to get to know another person better.

Regardless of what the dating pattern is, the same issues of dating apply. And these are things that are easy to master: How to get a date, how to be a date, how to learn from a date, and where to go from there. The basic rule of the dating game is that dating is relating. Understand how the game is played and you can succeed. Read on for all you need to know to get started.

Time Out

Try group dating. It is often much more fun and less stressful to go out with a group of friends together, especially if you know that the special person you want to be with will be there. You can often rely on friends for support, and it may be more comfortable than a first-time-couple encounter.

The Least You Need to Know

✧ The teen scene is the special playing field on which the dating game is played.

✧ Your society is different from previous generations.

✧ Teens in the past faced many of the same issues.

✧ Dating allows you to relate to another person.

✧ By relating to another person, you get to know yourself.

✧ The technological and communications revolution has changed some of the ways dating and relationships work.

15

Chapter 2

Everyone into the Game

In This Chapter

✧ You've got company

✧ Others have been there

✧ Everyone can play

✧ It's the best game—everyone can be a winner

Does it seem as if every other kid has this dating thing down—that you are the only one left out? Does it seem awkward to ask someone out? Everyone experiences this at first! Sometimes, even if you think of yourself as pretty savvy about this dating stuff, you may not know exactly how to approach someone new, and some of the same anxieties may arise.

Relax! This is all a part of what the dating game is all about. It is similar to what any game is all about: learning the rules of play and plunging right in. You need to play the game even if you're not an expert at it. Playing gives you practice, and with practice comes increased confidence. That's what I talk with you about in this chapter.

Get Ready, Get Set, Go!

The first and most important rule to keep in mind is that everyone—even the biggest stud or hottest chick at school—starts out as a beginner in the dating game. And, everyone begins at a different point in his or her life, with different experiences, perspectives, and goals in mind. However, despite these differences, you all have one thing in common: You all want to date and to date with ease!

As any good athlete can tell you, making something that's pretty difficult look easy requires a lot of practice, a bit of skill, and plenty of self-confidence. That's certainly true for dating. It's a game as well, a special game that has been played by girls and boys and men and women since the beginning of time. Although some of the rules may have changed, the fundamentals remain the same. Yes, believe it or not, the very same fundamentals that your parents observed when they began to think about dating still apply to your situation.

Time Out

Take some time to learn a few of the "dating fundamentals" I outline in this chapter. Although your goal may be to feel absolutely natural on a date, that feeling is something that only comes with knowledge and practice.

The Same Place, a Different Time

It's true that you're unique and special, and what happens to you is extremely personal and individual. But it might help you put your situation into perspective if you realize that throughout history, all teens have been in pretty much the same situation you face now—and someday your own children will be in the same position as well. All teens, including you, have to learn about dating—how to date, who to date, and how to make it feel right and natural.

Instant Replay

Monica, a 13-year-old, asked her parents how they met. Her mother told her that she had met her dad at a sweet-16 party when she was 15 and her dad was 16. They were from different schools but began to go to the movies together. Slowly they began to get to know each other, and by the age of 19 they decided to marry. This was quite a surprise to Monica, who had never really thought of her parents as teenagers like herself.

Take a good look at your mom and dad, aunts, uncles, and friends of your parents. I know it's hard to imagine, but they were teenagers, too—just your age and just as nervous and insecure about dating. Now, it's not that everything is the same. Your hair styles and fashion statements are certainly different, as are your tastes in music. However, no matter how dorky you think those fashions look now, you can bet that your parents thought they looked pretty cool. They made their mark on the world, and the world returned the favor; their teenage years were as important to them as yours are to you.

And remember: Your parents also had their own parents to deal with, complete with their own generation gaps, conflicts, and differences. You may think of your parents and grandparents as the same, as simply "the older generation."

Record Book

Much of the favorite music you enjoy today may seem
unique to you. But, the origin of new sounds and styles
may have their roots in the music of another generation.
Your parents may not have danced to rap music, but how
is the sound of 'N Sync really different from that of The
Beatles? The California melodies of The Beach Boys are still
around today, and many of you still find them great to listen and dance to.

But each grew up in a very different time, and faced as many
challenges in coping with one another as you face with your
parents.

It's Still the Same Old Story

What is most interesting about taking the time to think of
your parents as teenagers is the fact that they faced many of
the same challenges that you do today. They may not be willing to share this fact with you, but it's true! Everyone who
dates gets nervous, has fun, feels like a failure, enjoys success,
falls in love, gets hurt, feels frustrated—you name it! Some
emotions reoccur through the ages unchanged!

Am I Just Out of It?

Your parents aren't the only ones who may seem foreign to
you these days. Even your best friends and peers may change
so fast that you hardly know them. Some schoolmates appear
to grow taller by the second while others gain incredible

grace and athletic prowess in a very short time. Maybe you're one of those girls who has developed a woman's figure earlier than your peers, or maybe you're still waiting to blossom. Are you one of the boys who grows just a sprinkle of peach fuzz, or are you already shaving every day?

Time Out

Do this for fun. Sit down with your parents one day and ask them what they were like as teenagers. They might be shocked by the question, and, in turn, you might be pretty surprised at what you hear. Make sure you ask specifics: What music did they enjoy? Did they date a lot, or were they shy? Who knows, this might give you an entire new view of them, and it might cause them to think about you a little differently as well. Nothing creates stronger bonds than going through something together, or realizing how similar your experiences really are. One thing's for sure: You and your folks have more in common than you realize.

Everyone develops physically at a different pace. Social development is just as individual. You could be one of those 13-year-olds who seems to be absolutely at ease even in the most delicate situations, someone who can talk to anyone and get dates whenever they want. Or maybe you're one of those 15-year-olds who is still coming into your own and feels a bit shy, awkward, and hesitant in social situations. Does this mean that you're in dire need of help?

Well, we all need a little help sometimes, which is why I wrote this book. Keep in mind that even the sharpest, hippest kids didn't get to that comfortable place overnight—again, it takes practice. They may seem to be a little ahead of you in the dating game, but you can catch up as long as you get in the game!

Record Book

Sustaining self-confidence in social situations takes ongoing practice. You'll continue to learn new skills throughout your life. As you get older, you'll learn to fit into new workplaces, new neighborhoods, and new relationships of all kinds.

Let's Sort Things Out

Although you and your peers may be in slightly different places on the dating scale, you all have the same goal: to have fun dating and getting to know those people to whom you're attracted. Why should you date? Here are just a few of the most obvious reasons:

❖ Dating is fun.

❖ Dating offers you a chance to get to know someone better.

❖ Dating allows you to know yourself better.

❖ Dating helps you learn about life.

Despite how reasonable these goals are and how natural it must seem to want to be involved with people you like, dating is actually pretty hard—even though television and movies make it look easy. Fortunately, I can help you get started by giving you a few tips—which is what this book is all about.

Time Out

Look to older siblings and friends when you need help or advice. If you have some older friends who seem to know the score—maybe an older brother and sister—ask them (as one near-adult to another) how they gained their sense of what to do. They'll usually be flattered that you chose to ask them and proud to share with you some of the special lessons they've learned!

It Really Is a Game

You've heard the term, "the dating game," and it's actually good to think of dating as a game. And, like any other game, dating has its own fundamentals, rules, playing fields, referees, and culture. It has its own ways of keeping track of how you are doing and its own measures of success and opportunities for improvement.

The more you date, the more you'll learn about how to play the game. If you play a sport, think about what happens after you finish a game. The team and the coaches talk about the plays and discuss what you might have done differently. By doing so, you each gain some appreciation of your skills and shortcomings and pick up tips for improving your game. Use the same approach when it comes to playing the dating game. After each date, quickly review the event and see what you might do the same or differently to make the next date even more fun and relaxed. On the other hand, I don't mean to equate dating with athletic competition. For one thing, unlike most sports, dating doesn't require you to have some innate talent to excel. The remarkable thing about dating is that everyone can master the game; you don't have to be a particular type of person, physically or socially. You don't even have to be particularly coordinated or even that smart. Dating is the best type of game: Everyone can get into it, play as intensively as they want, have fun, and, *everyone* can succeed!

The Fundamentals of the Game

Like all games, dating has its own set of rules. We will talk about many of these rules as we discuss the basic elements of the date—asking someone out, having fun, and making it a worthwhile time. While these rules may seem to be a bit complicated, the fundamentals of the dating game are quite simple:

⬧ **The game is open to everyone.** Imagine an activity in which everyone can take part and improve the more they play. This is an activity which does not require any of the other players' permission to play. Dating is a game in which everyone is automatically invited to participate at whatever level they feel comfortable.

⬧ **You carry your own personality onto the field.** This is a game that's only requirement is that you bring your own unique personality and style onto the playing field. It is a part of the game. Who you are and how you look, act, think, and talk are the essential equipment you have, and your uniqueness is what makes the game so interesting! You don't wear uniforms in this game and you don't have to be a member of any team. This is an individual sport to which you bring all of who you are.

⬧ **You play when you like.** You can play this game whenever you like. There is no regularly scheduled playing time or practices. You can call the shots based on what you have going on and where you are in your life. And, if you stop playing for a while, you can resume the game whenever you want and pick up where you left off. You don't have to "use it or lose it!"

Record Book

Some of you may remember a television series called *The Dating Game.* It consisted of a guy trying to select a date out of a panel of three girls, or a girl attempting to choose a date from among three guys. The trick was that those selecting a date could only do so based on the contestants' voices and answers to certain questions. Nothing was really known about their personalities or appearances before they were chosen or rejected. Needless to say, more than a few contestants were surprised at the results!

✧ **Practice improves your game.** You're guaranteed to improve the more you participate in this activity. The more often you date, the more comfortable and accomplished you'll feel. The more often you gather up the nerve to ask someone out, the easier it gets the next time. And the more different kinds of dates you go on— picnics, dances, pizza parties, movies—the better you'll know how to show your date (and yourself) a good time!

✧ **The most successful game is when both parties win.** This is an unusual kind of game because the best result is that both parties win! Indeed, in the best of all possible worlds, no one would lose even one round in the dating game. But, as you may have discovered already, people get their hearts broken and their prides wounded—that just can't be helped. However, isn't it inspiring to know that you're not competing in this dating game, but cooperating so that everyone can have a good time and at the same time grow as individuals?

✧ **Dating is about relationships.** The sixth dating fundamental concerns establishing a relationship. A relationship is the ultimate goal of the game. This is what makes the game worthwhile—this is why people play the game. Dating is relating, and the dating game is all about relationships.

Penalty Flag

Play the dating game—don't play games with people. Treat your friends and dating partners with respect and honesty. Keep in mind that this game is not simply to score points at others' expense, where one party wins and one party loses. You're really in competition with yourself to see yourself improve.

It's a Game—Not a Race

Dating is one game in which there is no reward for speed. It simply does not matter if you are faster or slower than your friends. Sooner or later, you will all get to the finish line.

Know the Score

Do keep in mind that dating isn't about scoring points, or about "scoring." There is no opponent, no scoreboard, and no time limit. You can improve with every game you play, and if a mishap occurs, try to figure out what went wrong.

That's not to say you won't have a few bad dates. A few dates may even wind up being terrible. However, even a bad date can still yield some wins for both of you, for the wins are based on …

❖ How much you learned about your partner.

❖ How much you learned about yourself.

You may have had a dismal date, but you may still have come out ahead if you have realized why it wasn't successful.

Time Out

Aim for comfort, not for flash! Dating the hottest girl or hottest guy is one thing, but what you really want to get out of the dating game is the ease and confidence you need to ask out anyone who attracts you. It may take you a bit longer to reach that comfort level, but you will get there!

For the Love of the Game

Dating is a great way of keeping your enthusiasm high for life and for people. Face it—you have to eat lunch, and how much nicer it is to eat lunch with someone whom you really want to be with and get to know better! It is nice sometimes to be alone, but seeing a movie with a special friend is usually more fun.

In the chapters that follow, I'll give you some tips about the nuts and bolts of dating, including ...

❖ The rules you need to observe.

❖ The techniques you can learn.

❖ The variations you can adapt.

❖ The individual styles you can set.

In the end, what you'll learn about the most is you. You'll find out what makes you happy and who makes you happy. That is why dating is such a special kind of game that you'll probably find irresistible. What better way is there to learn more about yourself than by relating to another person and seeing how that other person relates to you?

Time Out

Relax! Although I suggest that you learn from your dating experiences, you don't have to dissect and analyze every dating encounter. Some dates are just about having fun with another person—without any seriousness.

The Least You Need to Know

✦ Everyone wants to date and starts at the same place—the beginning.

✦ People may be at different places in their level of experience.

✦ Parents and older siblings and friends have all been where you are—talk things over with someone who knows!

✦ The dating game has some universal fundamentals.

✦ Dating means learning about you.

Chapter 3

Your Relationship with Relationships

In This Chapter

✧ Relating and dating

✧ Your existing relationships

✧ Relating to yourself

In Chapter 2, "Everyone into the Game," you learned that the dating game has several important fundamentals. The sixth and most significant fundamental of the dating game is this: Dating is relating. Whether you are casually involved or exclusively linked, the way you date successfully is to make a relationship. To build and grow a relationship is what dating is meant for. That's just what we'll explore in this chapter.

Defining a Relationship

A relationship may sound like a simple enough concept. There is you and there is someone else; when you date, you create something between the two of you. It may seem that thinking about a "relationship" means you are considering something serious and heavy. But relationships don't have to be involved or complicated, although they sometimes are. On the other hand, they don't have to be trivial or superficial, although they sometimes are. You'll have a multitude of relationships with all different kinds of people—some romantic, some not; some successful, some not.

Time Out

Relationships don't have to be "heavy." Relationships are what any two people have in various degrees of togetherness. They establish a relationship simply by being involved.

What Are the Components of a Relationship?

Let's start by looking at a relationship in its simplest terms. A relationship is nothing more and nothing less than interaction between two or more people. And this can be any two people—not just people who are romantically involved.

The basic structure of a relationship consists of three elements:

✧ You

✧ Someone else

✧ Interaction

What you do in a relationship is to engage on some level with another person. And there are a lot of options for interaction, dating being just one of them, and—with the right person—one of the best ones. You can interact in many different ways and on many different terms, but, in essence, when you interact with someone you get to know them a little better. You can do so over the telephone, by e-mail, even the old-fashioned way—by letter. Pen pals from far-away places have relationships that can often last many years, and they often get to know each other well.

Time Out

If you think writing letters doesn't have charm, watch the movie *84 Charing Cross Road,* a film that chronicles a re-markable friendship between a man and a woman over many years. They learned about each other's lives, families, dreams, and thoughts from 30 years of writing letters. These two people actually knew each other as well as if they had spent every weekend together. Although they never actu-ally met face-to-face, they enjoyed the deepest of rela-tionships.

Why Have Relationships?

Relationships are natural. As you converse with others over insignificant things like homework assignments and cafeteria menus, you begin to get to know something about each other. As humans, we need other people in our lives to add a richness that we cannot achieve alone.

Sociologists and anthropologists tell us that man is indeed a social animal—being with others is just a part of our basic na-ture.

Furthermore, relationships are fun. Everyone you meet is dif-ferent, even if they appear on the surface to be pretty similar. The great thing about going to parties and other social gath-erings is that it gives you the opportunity to meet someone new and unique. You should view a party as something that's fun—a continuous set of surprises.

Relationships Have Their Own Lives

Now it's important to stress that relationships of all kinds take work—they don't simply flourish on their own. In order for a relationship to grow, both parties need to actively participate. For example, there needs to be basic communication, and communication is a two-way street. There are friendships that have been maintained for many years because of the efforts each friend makes. Parties usually bring into a relationship their own techniques for growing it and keeping it alive. In Chapter 4, "Building a Relationship," you will learn some techniques you might find helpful in starting a relationship and keeping it going.

All relationships have a beginning, a middle, and most have an end. The end may include a dramatic uproar, complete with yelling and tears, or it may end in a calm whisper. Even if a relationship does continue throughout your life, it will change along the way because you or your friend will change. You'll end up in a different place—geographically or emotionally. In addition, as you grow and change, so will your needs for companionship. At some point, it will be natural for you to question whether your relationship is important to you any longer.

Time Out

Think of a party as a relationship-making adventure. A party may have great music, great food, and even a great setting, but what really makes or breaks a party is the people. Parties let you work on old relationships as well as establish new ones. Observe each person in the room and try to figure out what makes him or her unique.

"Real-ationships"

I think of relationships as being fundamental to what the dating game is all about. But there are relationships, and there are what I like to call "real-ationships"—those relationships that are simply filled to the brim with the right stuff.

Among the goals of any positive relationship is to share in the pleasure of both the friendship and the things you have in common—including the way you see the world. Positive relationships are more than just fun. They allow us to appreciate the joy that comes from companionship. Although it's nice to be alone at times, everyone needs the warmth and stimulation of human interaction. You learn from hearing what others think and feel: Watching a movie with someone may not influence how you see it as it unfolds before you, but discussing the film afterward expands your experience.

Instant Replay

Dennis and Susan were high school sweethearts who dated during their junior and senior years. However, Dennis was interested in spending more time with his guy friends and really did not want to get serious. They gradually drifted apart—each went to different colleges, got involved with other people, and entered the working world. However, a chance meeting when they were both 28 brought them together again. This time, they were very compatible and in similar circumstances. Dennis and Susan were both somewhat different people than they were 10 years earlier. They were not new people in one sense, but they were very new people in another, so they were able to connect in a whole different way. A romance bloomed, and they've stayed together to this day.

Even bad relationships can be real-ationships, if they give you something you can learn from. And what you learn is how to—and maybe how not to—build and keep a relationship.

You Already Have Experience with Relationships

Although you may not have dated much yet, you have had plenty of experience with relationships: You've got parents, maybe brothers and sisters, friends, classmates, and neighbors. Clearly, not all your relationships are romantic ones, and some of them may actually even be unpleasant, but they are relationships nonetheless. Dates, on the other hand, are special kinds of relationships, rooted in the desire to be with a special person and see if romance can bloom.

Some of your relationships are more intense than others—usually, you'll have a more intense relationship with a friend who has been a buddy of yours since second grade than you do with someone you just met this year. However, the length of time you've known someone doesn't always determine how deep your relationship goes. You may have experienced very quickly becoming best friends with someone you've just met—almost without effort!

Penalty Flag

Don't take friendships for granted. They have to be nurtured and cared for; they are precious.

Relations with Relations

Since this is a book about dating, you're probably concentrating on potentially romantic relationships. However, it's also important to recognize the relationships you have with the members of your family, including parents, brothers, sisters, stepparents, and any others with whom you have quite significant relationships. These relationships influence who you are—and, believe it or not, who you date. Consider your relationship with your parents. You certainly have a different kind of relationship with your mother now than when you were five years old. Back then you needed your mom more to do basic things for you—even help feed you. Now that you're pretty independent, your relationship with your mom has changed (even if you do still expect her to buy and cook the food). You and your mom aren't necessarily more distant than you were when you were younger, but the relationship certainly has changed as you've matured. The same can be said of relationships with your brothers and sisters, who have grown up along with you.

You interact with your family as you grow up, and at each stage you see them and they see you differently. To you, it probably seems as if you're always entering a new phase with your family members, but at the same time, it may be difficult for them to see you as anything but a child frozen at a particular age.

Relationships with Former Relationships

Another group of people you may relate to are those "old flames"—people you've dated in the past but now no longer see. You meet someone, you relate to someone, you date someone, and you break up. This happens all the time. This may be the end of the dating, but this is not necessarily the end of the relationship. You'll always have a relationship with the person, even if you're no longer involved. You'll have a relationship with what was! Old relationships form a part of who you are because who you are is influenced by all the people you've met along the way.

Time Out

Look on the positive side. No matter how bad a date is (your date may not laugh at your jokes and you may be bored enough to look at your watch every five minutes), you still have a chance to make it worth your while. Just think about what went wrong with your choice of a date, or your own attitude, and you're bound to make better choices next time out!

You've Got a Friend

In addition to being among the most important and longest-lasting relationships in your life, friendships may also offer a solid foundation for a romantic involvement. There's nothing like being best friends with the person you love most (in a romantic way).

Sally, a 13-year-old girl, remembers when a boy from junior high school came to her house for a visit. "I was so excited. We talked and laughed in the kitchen. It was the first time I had been alone with a boy. We were joking around; I liked him so much. Somehow we got crazy and I accidentally poured some of my mom's leftover potato soup over his head. Here I was, this serious junior high school girl trying to impress this guy, but this first experience of being alone with a boy just seemed to change my personality. Luckily, he just licked his lips and laughed along with me." What was important to Sally was that they remained friends. She took a good deal of comfort in that fact that her clumsiness was perceived as friendly.

As Sally discovered, the best romantic or dating relationships are the ones that have friendship at their roots. Successful couples talk about their partners as being their "best friends." What this means is that they have grown to feel as if they can be themselves when they are together, they are there for one another, and they can savor the value of having someone else truly concerned about their own well-being. This kind of relationship takes time and care to form and maintain, which is why your parents and older siblings will tell you—over and over again—to take your time when it comes to forming romantic relationships!

Penalty Flag

Don't worry if a relationship changes, or even ends. Keep in mind that relationships have a cycle: They begin, they evolve, and they sometimes end. You may have to accept the fact that a particular relationship has changed along the way, and it may not be as meaningful to you now as it once was. This happens to everyone, and you just have to accept it at times.

You Have a Relationship with Yourself

Maybe you've heard the expression, "Be your own best friend." Well, there isn't any better advice I can give you. Before you can form significant relationships with your peers, you've got to get to know and like yourself. Do you like being in your own company? Have you found hobbies or interests that intrigue you? It's as important to learn to relate to yourself as it is to others, and the sooner you manage that task, the better! Now, that's not to say that you need to constantly examine how you feel about yourself—you'd only bore yourself and your friends by doing this. But understanding how unique you are and what particular qualities you bring to all of your relationships, and then projecting that to others, is the best way to attract the right kind of people. Dating is setting up a relationship as a two-way street: You want to learn about someone else and you also want someone else to learn about you.

Instant Replay

Joe is now 21 but thinks it's great that he, his parents, and his two brothers keep getting closer as they grow up together. When he and his brothers were younger, the three years that separated each of them seemed vast, and Joe often felt that he had nothing in common with them (especially when his brothers were 11 and 14, and he was 17). But the age difference melted away when they all became young adults and faced similar concerns; Joe found he was closer friends with his brothers as they grew up.

In the next chapter, we will explore the techniques for starting a relationship and keeping it going.

Penalty Flag

Don't forget to move on! The more you date, the more you'll break up, so it's best to learn how to shake it off as quickly as possible. That's not to say that a feeling of loss isn't natural, especially if breaking up wasn't your idea to begin with. But remember, that was then and this is now. It's good to have had these experiences and marvelous to have learned from them. But it's important to recognize that it's time to move on and to welcome the new.

The Least You Need to Know

- ✧ A significant fundamental of dating is the development of relationships.

- ✧ Both good and bad relationships can be positive experiences if you learn something from them.

- ✧ Your experience forming and maintaining relationships with your family and friends helps you form romantic dating relationships.

- ✧ Getting to know and like yourself first helps you attract the right kind of people.

Chapter 4

Building a Relationship

In This Chapter

✧ Relationships begin with you

✧ Choosing your friends, your dates

✧ Techniques for meeting new people

✧ Techniques for keeping relationships going

As I've said before and I'll say again—dating means relating. That means having the guts to meet a new person, learn to talk about yourself, ask questions of the person you're with, and listen—really listen—to his or her answers. Easier said than done, right? You may feel awkward about approaching new people and starting to talk, or you may even feel unsure of which new people you really want to know better. And, talking to a new person—especially one of the opposite sex—can be really scary!

The good news is that each of these challenges will become easier to overcome the more often you try. And, because dating is based on establishing a relationship, the better you become at building relationships, the greater success you'll have dating.

In this chapter, I will help you figure out who you are so that you'll feel more secure in this strange world of dating and have something special to bring to the new relationships you hope to build. Like everything else worthwhile, dating requires a bit of learning and practice. But, just as you work out regularly to keep in shape for the game, dating will soon become a part of your everyday life.

Knowing Yourself

Although it may sound strange, the first person you need to look at when you're about to build a new relationship is you. Ignore your first instinct, which is probably to fixate on your shortcomings, only focusing on the fact that you could be better looking, better organized, smoother, taller, less klutzy, and so on. Instead, think hard about your good qualities. What do your friends like about you? Your siblings? Your parents?

Penalty Flag

Avoid projecting a negative image of yourself to the world. Most people are naturally attracted to those who have a strong and positive sense of themselves. Concentrate on your positive qualities as much as you can, without bragging or appearing conceited.

Now, that's not to say you should ignore your faults completely. You've just got to look at yourself with some objectivity. While you might not be so great at meeting new people or reining in the bad jokes you can't seem to help telling, re-mind yourself that you're great at math or a terrific soccer player.

Here's something that might help you figure out your pluses and evaluate your minuses. Many business leaders use this technique to evaluate their management style, but it also works well for personal issues. Take a piece of paper and cre-ate two columns, one with the heading "My Positives" and the second "Things to Work On." Then, take a few minutes to step outside of yourself and pretend you're a third person there to observe your behavior.

- ✧ In the left-hand column, list all the positives about yourself and your personality.

- ✧ In the right-hand column, list all the negatives that you would like to change.

- ✧ Under each of the entries, compose an action plan to emphasize the pluses and an action plan to de-empha-size (or eliminate) the minuses.

- ✧ Re-evaluate both lists regularly about every three to six months.

While it is often difficult to be objective about yourself, there is something very satisfying about taking some quiet time and looking at yourself with open eyes now and then. After all, who else knows you better than you do?

Knowing What Kind of Friend You Want

Now that you've got some sense of who you are and what you can bring to a dating relationship, it's time to think about whom you might like to bring into your life. When you imagine yourself dating, you probably picture yourself with some gorgeous hunk of a man or woman. But, before you get carried away, your best bet is to think more about friendship than romance. Friendship is where it all starts, be-lieve me. You need to ask yourself what kind of friend you are looking for—and ask yourself why.

The kind of friend you want to be is very dependent on what you want another friend to be to you. How are you as a friend to others? That determines what kind of friend you want to be.

Time Out

Think for a moment about the popular television show *Friends*. A group of friends (three guys and three girls) engages in many funny scenes together. They seem to share a constant party. Sure they have their moments, but they always seem to be perfectly humorous and engaging with one another. But we see a show, and only 30 minutes at best. Friendships are constant and complex, and they require much in the way of human interaction.

What are friends for? Everyone defines this a little differently. Some people require friends to be totally devoted and always available. Some people purely and simply want a friend to "be there" for them on occasion. Some people are overjoyed just knowing their friends exist, but do not require them to be constant companions. The significant thing here is to think about what works for you. Do you need a best friend? Do you want a friend to talk to—and do you want to talk about serious and important things or just small talk? None of these is the right or wrong way to look at friendship. You need to look at this in your own style in the same way you assessed yourself.

Now, look at the friends you've already made. Are some of them not exactly what you had in mind? Do you expect more out of a friend than you are presently getting? Are your friends expecting more out of you than you can give?

Penalty Flag

Don't assume too much about a friendship at the start. Often, what gets in the way of building a strong relationship with a new person is that you each have very different expectations about what kind of friendship you want. For example, if you want an exclusive, one-on-one relationship with a person who likes to keep things loose, you'll need to revise your goals if you want the relationship to continue.

Knowing What Kind of Friend You Want to Be

There is an old saying that states "you need to be a friend in order to have a friend." Here is an opportunity for you to examine your own objectives and see if you can bring into a friendship the same things you require of others. At the very least, you need to understand whether your expectations of a friendship are different from others'.

This is not a difficult task. Usually, you think about friends as people who share common interests or have interesting differences. This only requires you to look at yourself in terms of friendship and think about your requirements:

- ✧ What do you want in a friend?
- ✧ Are there people in your group you would want as friends?
- ✧ Are there people outside your group with whom you would like to be friends?

This is not to say that friendships can't evolve. You may be one of someone's group of best friends, but in time may move to a more exclusive relationship—just because it most often seems it is more pleasurable doing things together than with others.

Instant Replay

One of the jokes from an ex-vaudevillian, my father-in-law, tells something about the permanency of some friend-ships. There are two comedian buddies, Dave and Bob. Dave to Bob: "We're friends to the end!" Bob to Dave: "Lend me five dollars!" Dave to Bob: "This is the end!"

Questioning Your Friendships

In most cases, friendship has a degree of equality about it, a sense of mutual admiration and enjoyment for one another. That's not to say that everything between you has to be ab-solutely equal, but a friendship that is completely one-sided is usually pretty upsetting to at least one of the parties, often both. The person who wants more out of the friendship may feel slighted or even used by someone who's less attached.

What should you do if you have friends who have expecta-tions that don't match your own? You have four choices:

✧ Change your expectations.

✧ Encourage them to change their expectations.

✧ Accept the friendship "as is" and treasure it for what it brings into your life.

✧ Move on.

What's most important is that you don't compromise your values or goals or repress an important part of your personality in order to establish a friendship with someone. Choosing friends and building relationships is a lifelong process, and you'll have to experiment quite a bit to see what works for you.

Penalty Flag

Don't expect others to change for you. However, you might find that, in a relationship, both you and the other person are influenced by one another and change at least a little in response to that influence. In fact, the best friendships involve this kind of give and take, so don't give up if at first you're on slightly different wavelengths.

There is always the issue of popularity and cliques. Every school has them. Are you in the "in crowd" or do you want to be? How much do you care about that?

Have you ever thought about what makes other kids popular? Usually, others regard them as leaders because they ...

- ✧ Look good.
- ✧ Are good at sports.
- ✧ Display self-confidence.
- ✧ Are smart.
- ✧ Know how to be or appear "cool."
- ✧ Have a great personality.
- ✧ Dress well.
- ✧ Know how to make friends.

These qualities certainly help to attract others, but many of them are not necessary when it comes to building new friendships or establishing dating relationships—and that's something you need to keep in mind. If being one of the "in crowd" is important to you and you aren't quite there yet, think again about letting the world see your best qualities. Put yourself out there, let yourself shine, and you may become more popular faster than you think possible.

In the meantime, you need to learn about the fine art of communication—the single most important skill to have when it comes to dating.

Friendships and Communications

One of the joys of having friends is being able to talk to them about many things. Communication is critical in establishing and keeping friendships. But communication is a two-way street. You have to be both a good talker and a good listener.

The Gift of Gab

Talking and listening are the basics of communication, but most people aren't particularly skilled at one or the other. The good news is that you can train yourself to be an expert in these two elements of communication.

Without question, being able to go up and talk to someone you don't know may be hard at first, especially if you're somewhat shy or unaccustomed to meeting new people. However, talking is the only way you have to communicate. It's the way you ...

⬧ Introduce yourself to someone else.

⬧ Find out about another person's interests.

⬧ Keep the momentum of a growing relationship going.

Clearly, you're going to need to learn to open your mouth and say what you mean if you're going to get anywhere in either the friendship or the dating world.

Instant Replay

Chris, 16, used to feel awkward about going up and talking to people—even someone he knew. After taking an acting class in school, he began to imagine starting a conversation as he would if he were an actor reciting lines from a play. His lines would be pretty simple: "Hi, I'm Chris Smith, and I just wanted to say hello! I saw you working hard in English class today!" By being simple and direct, the girl he met didn't regard his approach as anything other than a friendly greeting from someone who was interested in meeting her. Chris figured the worst-case scenario was that the relationship would go no further, in which case he'd be no worse off than if he hadn't spoken to her at all. In fact, he would often find himself with a date with a girl he had wanted to get to know better!

First, introducing yourself to someone doesn't have to be clever or smooth—in fact, the more direct you are, the better.

Some people pay attention to clever "pick up" lines. In fact, some guys, and even some girls, pride themselves on the importance of having some witty opening statement to captivate someone in whom they are interested. "Pick up" lines aren't necessary, but if you want, you can rehearse some special remark—just understand that it needs to be "you."

Once the ice is broken, know the next thing you'd like to say, preferably something that shows you've noticed some quality about the person you're meeting. I like a method I call the statement-question technique, which you can say in either order. Take a look at some examples:

- ◆ You seem to be very good in Spanish. (statement) Are you interested in going to Mexico or Spain one day? (question)

- ◆ I heard a great new Backstreet Boys CD. (statement) Do you like them? (question)

- ◆ Doesn't school seem like it's getting harder? (question) It seems like I have more homework. (statement)

Using this technique not only shows what you're thinking about, but also immediately involves the person you're meeting in the conversation.

All people like being asked about themselves (as long as you are not too nosy at first). Remember that most people will be flattered that you've singled them out because you find them interesting, even intriguing. The worst that can happen is that the person ignores you, which won't be pleasant; but, because he or she had never been a part of your life before, you'll get over it pretty quickly!

The Art of Listening

The best tip I can give you is to learn to be a good listener. It's a skill that will help you make and keep friends, create positive dating relationships, and even excel at school and, eventually, in the workplace. If you don't listen, you can't possibly learn anything about other people or the world around you.

You know how it is. Doesn't it make all the difference in the world when the person you're talking to really listens to what you say and cares about your opinions and ideas? Well, you're not alone. The person you want to date feels the very same way, and the quickest way to his or her heart is to listen carefully.

The trick is not only to listen, but to *look* like you're listening. If your eyes are flitting about the room, he or she will probably think you're distracted and inattentive. Fix your gaze on his or her eyes and stay focused for the best results.

Apart from learning important things about the person with whom you're conversing, by listening you'll also be able to take your cues for the next step in the conversation from what he or she says. The best rule of thumb is to follow his or her lead—at least at first. If you started the conversation by asking about school, but your new acquaintance brings up next Friday's dance, go with the flow. (It might even be a hint about a potential date!)

Of course, you can interject using the statement-question technique whenever there is a lull or it seems the conversation has shifted to your side. Just remember the statement-question format. For example, if your partner has answered your question in a statement or a question, simply give a short statement about what the partner said (statement), then ask a follow-up question to keep the topic going (question). The statement part lets the partner know how you feel about the subject (which provides him or her with important information about who you are), and by asking another question, you keep things moving along.

Making Friends Who Are Different Than You

Although you want to keep the level of the friendship pretty equal, you should feel free to make friends and have dating relationships with all kinds of people, especially in your teen years when you're still finding out who you really are. Feel free to branch out and explore relationships with people from different economic and ethnic circles, and certainly make it a point to seek out people who have different interests and hobbies than you do. Nothing is more exciting than learning something new from a peer who's experienced and interested in that particular subject.

Recall that one of the dating fundamentals is that dating is a democratic activity—the game is open to everyone. You'll learn more about yourself and other people if you do not restrict yourself to only developing friendships with people who are just like you. That goes for dating as well: Especially at the start, you may be more comfortable dating someone who has a similar background to your own. But you still can develop friendships with a host of others who have different interests.

Time Out

Try to engage in relationships with people from other backgrounds; this opens your experience to different cultures, foods, and customs. Our country is not exactly a melting pot any more; people now often want to maintain their own traditions as well as become part of the whole. What a great opportunity to learn about others!

Sustaining a Relationship

Once you've started a relationship with a new person, you'll probably need to spend some time and energy to keep it going. Relationships may have lives of their own, but they require effort to keep building and refreshing them. There is a basic principle for sustaining a relationship: Never take someone for granted.

It's important that both of you are conscious of what you're trying to build; a friendship or dating relationship is very much a dual effort. Relationships may grow routine as time goes on. Try new things and explore different ways of having fun with your friend. Talk about new subjects and share your inner thoughts, but never assume that just because you are in a relationship (friends or the dating kind), it will last indefinitely. Both people need to stay actively involved in order for the relationship to work long-term.

Changing Relationships

You'll be making friends and establishing and sustaining relationships for the rest of your life. You might have the same
friends for many years, or your friendships might change
fairly often. That's a highly individual matter. But remember,
every relationship is not a measure of your own self-worth or
that of your partner. Relationships change—that is the nature
of the beast. But sometimes relationships get better!

Penalty Flag

Don't assume that it's your fault or it's because you're un-
worthy if a relationship changes or fades away. Most of the
time, it's no one's fault when a relationship doesn't work
out. It just means that two people who once thought they
had a lot in common realize that they're no longer compatible. When it happens to you—and it will—accept it and
move on. If you can learn something about your own behavior and how to better sustain a relationship, all the
better.

In the end, you have to pay attention to relationships. You
may need to reassess where you are and who you are and see
if this person meets those requirements. If they do, treat the
relationship with respect and try continually to delight the
other person. Some relationships last a few days and others
can last a lifetime. Even the brief ones can give you great insight into what you wish to get out of life and what makes
you happy.

After considering the teen scene, realizing that everyone is
in the dating game, and exploring the fundamentals of the

dating game, it's now time to plunge into the mechanics of the dating game itself. In the chapters that follow, you'll learn more about beginning, sustaining, and ending a dating relationship.

The Least You Need to Know

✧ Knowing yourself is a key to starting and maintaining good relationships.

✧ Learning how to maintain friendships is a good way to learn how to form significant dating relationships.

✧ Compromising your values and goals or changing your personality to fit another's are bad for you and your relationships.

✧ Talking and listening are critical skills in developing and maintaining relationships.

✧ Measuring your self-worth by whether you sustain a relationship is wrong.

Part 2
The Dating Game

Ben is now ready to start to play the game. He pauses to think about how he can summon up the courage to make that telephone call. And after that—should she say "yes"—he needs to know how to converse with her and how to keep the date moving. What should he expect of a date? Does every date end up being a serious relationship? How can he break up if he needs to?

In this part, I'll show you the techniques of the game and the rules of play. You'll learn the basics of asking someone out, what kinds of dates you might enjoy, techniques for keeping the conversation going, and how a relationship evolves into something serious. The concluding chapter in this part will consider the challenge of breaking up.

Chapter 5

Asking for a Date

In This Chapter

✧ Knowing what a date is

✧ Knowing what a date isn't

✧ Asking someone out

✧ Being asked out

So now you're ready for the big moment. It's time to ask out the person you've been thinking about for a long time. You are finally acting on what you've wanted to do for a long time. You probably haven't just been thinking about this— you've been dreaming about it. You are ready for the big invitation. In this chapter, I'll show you how to get through the big moment and on with the date!

Getting Up for the Game

You reach for the telephone to call. You rehearse many times speaking into the turned-off portable phone; you listen to your words and intonation. You even look at yourself in the mirror and watch your expression as you say the magic

words—even though you'll be on the telephone and your potential date-to-be won't even see your face. You've got the
script down pat. You sound smooth! You're finally ready to
turn the phone on and dial. The telephone rings on the
other end.

Wait a second! What if a parent answers the phone? Even
worse, what if your intended does? What if he or she thinks
you're a nerd, or un-cool, or awkward? What if he or she
thinks you're way out of your league and not only won't
they go out with you, they won't even talk to you? What if
the girl or guy you've been thinking about for weeks hasn't
given you a single thought?

Your hands begin to sweat. Suddenly, the moment you've
been looking forward to with such excitement seems to be
one of terror! What if that special someone simply hangs up
the phone? Are you going to feel horrible and look stupid the
next day at school when everyone knows what happened? Is
this really such a good idea? Maybe it's too soon. After all,
there is no need to rush. Maybe this isn't the perfect time.
Hey, what's wrong with calling back a little later? Maybe
they're having dinner late and this isn't the best time to talk!

Someone answers the phone. You hear "Hello!" You recognize that voice and begin to speak.

Time Out

Stay as calm as you can when you call for a date, but remember that most people are just as nervous as you at this
point. And remember: Chances are, the person you're asking is nervous, too, and his or her reaction might reflect
that. If he or she sounds hesitant or reluctant at first, it
might be that he or she is just as excited as you are!

The other end of the phone may have some mystery for you. You simply may not know what that other person is experiencing. There are three ways to deal with some of the anxiety the call may elicit. You can visualize that the person is as pleased to hear from you as you are to call them. Or you can assume the role of a confident conversationalist as an actor would. What you need to keep in mind is that, at the end of the day, a date isn't such a big deal after all.

Defining a Date

Let's relax a bit and begin by defining what a date is. Don't think of it as a final examination on which your entire grade is based—you'll have lots of opportunities to prove yourself to this person and any number of others. A date—especially a first date—is simply an occasion to be with someone else for a certain amount of time and for a certain amount of pleasant, personal interaction. It is no different than deciding to meet a friend at a designated place and time.

On the other hand, if you're the one doing the asking, it's almost impossible not to feel that an acceptance or rejection is a direct reflection on you as a person. The truth is that there are many reasons why someone may choose not to accept your request for a date. The time may not be convenient, they may already be busy, or they may be involved with someone else. As a matter of fact, it may have absolutely nothing to do with you at all.

This Is a New Relationship!

A date is also the beginning of a new relationship. Of course, you may already feel connected in some way to this new person. You may have interacted in class with him or her, worked on the school newspaper together, talked, and shared a laugh. But going on a date is different; now you are making a statement to someone that you would like to get to know him or her better. And you would also like him or her to know you better.

Instant Replay

Sometimes, even people interested in accepting a date have to say no, and they're genuinely sorry when they do. For instance, Laurie, 17, was madly interested in a new boy, but she was already in a relationship with another guy. She felt she would be betraying her boyfriend if she accepted. The new boy could not understand that her rejection really had nothing to do with him—it was because she didn't feel right doing what she wanted to do. However, her feelings convinced her that her present relationship was probably not right for her if she was interested in going out with someone else.

There is something about a date—the question (asking) and the answer (accepting)—that signals to both of you that you're taking this relationship to a different level. You want to be with someone and he or she wants to be with you; by your asking and his or her accepting, you both confirm that this is the case.

But the greatest thing about dating is that you get to move a relationship along by having fun! The object of a date is to get to know someone better, allow someone to get to know you better, and have a fun time doing it together.

We Have a Match!

Sometimes we select people to ask out because of their looks or their personality. We might choose someone because they are interesting or entertaining, or because of their lifestyle. However, sometimes we really don't know why we choose a particular person.

What exactly attracts you to another person is often a mystery, and it's always unique to you. The very things that attract you to someone are things that may turn off your best friend.

It is good, however, to think about why you choose the people you do. It could be their looks—and there's nothing wrong with that (in fact, it's almost impossible to be attracted to someone without some kind of physical chemistry going on) as long as they've got other things that interest you. Think about what else there is: A good sense of humor? A passion for the same hobby you love? The more accurate you can be, the more you'll learn about yourself when it comes to dating.

Instant Replay

A 16-year-old boy named Mark had a first date with someone he had really wanted to ask out for a long time. He came back from his date and telephoned his best friend, sort of amazed. "You know, it was nice being with her and all, although it wasn't that romantic. But, the most awesome thing was that I had such fun being with her!" This is the stuff that can lead to memories of enchantment as much as full moons and soft music. The fact is that dating is important for the fun it brings into a relationship.

Asking Her Out: The Male Perspective

So now it's time. How do you do it? There are really only three ways to do the asking, and with each of the approaches, the end result is the same: You ask the person to go out with you. Let us consider ...

✧ The direct approach.

✧ The conversational approach.

✧ The long-lead approach.

Record Book

In 1986, sociologist S. R. Jorgensen asked 1,135 college students what they sought in someone to date. The ranking order from greatest down were: physical attractiveness, personality, humor, intelligence, manners, sincerity, compatible interests, conversational ability, and being fun.

Although you can certainly ask someone out by written invitation via letter, note, or e-mail, we're going to concentrate on verbal communication. Not only is this approach by far the most common, it's also the most challenging.

The direct approach is the most uncomplicated. In essence, what you do is approach a young woman, simply say, "Hi!" and ask her a single question: "Will you go out with me?" Now, the question can be worded differently, but the end is the same. Variations include ...

✧ "Hi. I have two tickets to the football game on Friday. Would you like to go with me?"

✧ "Hi. I'd like to see the new movie that's opening this weekend. Would you like to join me?"

✧ "Hey. I wonder if we could go out together on Saturday night?"

Record Book

In 1983, the Roper Organization, a well-known opinion research firm, asked people what they first noticed in the physical characteristics of a person. Men noticed a woman's figure first, face second, clothes third, and smile fourth. Women noticed how a man was dressed first, his eyes second, his build third, and his face and smile tied for fourth.

If you ask over the telephone, you can get over any nervousness about making conversation by plunging right into the reason for the call—after, of course, you have introduced yourself and made some chit-chat about school or how your potential date is doing that day. Then just plunge in: "I'd like to ask you out on Friday night. How about a movie?" This way, you get to the point pretty quickly, which means you can avoid confusion or awkward pauses in the conversation.

Your response to your potential date depends on the answer you get:

- ✧ She accepts. You name a time and place to meet.

- ✧ Your potential date declines, saying that she's busy. If you have another day in mind, go ahead and ask.

- ✧ She declines your second offer as well. She may indeed still be busy. Now it's time to ask her if you may call again. If the answer is yes, call again in a week or so and see what happens. If you get another "no" answer, you might want to reconsider calling again. Instead, suggest that your potential date call you whenever she's free.

Time Out

When it comes to optimizing your chances for an acceptance, be specific and ask in advance. Don't call on Thursday and ask, "Are you free sometime this weekend?" because some people don't want to seem too available. Ask about a specific day and, if that doesn't work out, have another option available.

The direct approach is really a straightforward interchange involving a few short questions: "Will you go out with me?" and, if necessary, "How about another time?" It requires little build-up, is very businesslike, and allows you to get to the point quickly.

The conversational approach requires a little preparation. In this scenario, you talk to her on the phone about things other than a date while easing into the question. If you take this approach, it's best to have two or three topics in mind. The first may be something related to the present day—what happened in school in a mutual class, how your homework load is going, whether you saw a cool show on TV that night, etc. Then, move the topic to something related to a date—such as a musical group or movie you want to take her to see. See if she shares an interest in this group. When she seems to be interested, then ask the question: "Would you like to go with me?" You then proceed to the option of alternative dates if necessary.

The conversational approach lets you ease into the date question and is especially useful if you don't really know her well and wish to gauge her interest in you as well as the date. If you don't have anything in mind for the date (like a concert or a particular movie), keep the discussion general and wind up by saying something like, "You know, I've enjoyed talking with you. Would you like to go out and do something with me Saturday night?" If she inquires what you had in mind, continue to be casual; you might respond: "Oh, just get a hamburger and talk." You've offered her the option of regarding the date as just a continuation of the current conversation rather than a big romantic adventure.

Penalty Flag

Don't be down just because you were not successful. It's true that you're bound to ask someone out who just isn't interested in you. But think of how many people might think you're cute whom you just don't care for. It's a two-way street—one filled with opportunities.

The long-lead approach is similar to the conversational approach. In this case, you're aiming to have several casual conversations before you ask the young woman out. This technique works best if the two of you don't know each other very well. The conversations allow you to warm up to each other and introduce topics that you both find interesting, which will make the actual date more fun and relaxed. Have in mind a list of things in which you have an interest. Here are a few ideas:

- ✧ Favorite subjects in school
- ✧ Teachers you have liked and disliked
- ✧ School activities
- ✧ Movies and movie stars
- ✧ Music videos and CDs
- ✧ Musical groups
- ✧ Sports

Instant Replay

Eighteen-year-old David spent his second date with a beautiful but sort of boring girl at a comedy club. The co-median was not great, but David was aware that only he and another woman a couple of tables away were consis-tently laughing heartily at the same jokes. His date didn't get any of the humor. David managed to speak to the woman who laughed along with him and got her name and telephone number. And the rest, as they say, is history! He quickly recognized the importance he placed on "laugh compatibility," which made her incredibly attractive to him.

These are all easy enough subjects to talk about. Just make sure you have an opinion and that you ask your potential date her opinion in return. Keep in mind the statement-question method of approaching conversation outlined in Chapter 4, "Building a Relationship":

- ✦ I have Mr. Fine for biology this year; he is really a great teacher. (statement) Who do you have? (question)

- ✦ I think the new Britney Spears video is awesome. (state-ment) Do you like her music? (question)

Each of these statements easily leads you into a casual con-versation. After this conversation or after a series of conversa-tions about this or additional topics, you may then pose the dating question: "I've really liked talking to you. Would you like to go out with me on Saturday?"

There are times in which you go out on a date without having spoken to the person at all beforehand. You may have been set up by friends who think you might like each other. On these occasions, you have to use the conversational techniques outlined above to explore your interests. Just have a statement or two about several topics ready, and remember the statement—question techniques. You need to regard "blind dates" as part of the adventure of the dating game: You never really know who she is until you meet her.

Regardless of the approach you take, the end result is always the same: You ask someone to meet you in order to continue your conversation, a conversation that forms the basis of your relationship. The outcome of this is yes, no, or deferred (sort of like college decisions). But, the absolute worst thing that can happen is that she doesn't want to go out with you.

Instant Replay

One of my favorite stories relates to the 16-year-old son of a friend, who was set up with a girl by a distant friend who thought of their mutual interest in old Beach Boys music. He called her and they talked for over an hour on the phone, after which he asked her to go out. But the remarkable thing about this was that after the hour-long conversation, he realized he had gotten absolutely no more information about her other than that she loved The Beach Boys; he didn't know where she went to school, what her other interests were, or whether she was involved with someone else. The conversation itself was so absorbing that it kept going and going—stimulating an increasing interest by both parties to date, if only to find out more!

In this case, you're no worse off than before when you weren't going out with her. Nothing ventured, nothing gained!

Asking Him Out: The Female Perspective

Can you ask him out? Is there a rule against this? In a way, that's up to you. If you're a female teenager in the twenty-first century, the only rule is that you do what makes you feel comfortable emotionally, physically, and socially.

Time Out

No matter what happens, take the situation for what it is. Every time you ask someone out, you get better at asking someone out. Even if he or she declines, you get practice in taking the plunge, and it becomes more familiar to you the next time around.

Making the first move pleases some young men and scares others away. Some find it flattering. It means that they're not always the "chasers," and implies that someone is really interested in them. Some guys really admire someone who is "gutsy" and aggressive enough to ask outright for what they really want. It also gives guys the opportunity of being on the other end of the phone and seeing what the experience is like to be the person asked rather than the "asker."

The techniques for girls asking boys out are identical to those we listed for boys asking girls. You can use the direct approach, the conversational approach, or the long-lead approach. The important thing to understand is that what works for boys usually works for girls as well.

Instant Replay

Jenny, 15, states: "When I was 13, I had to invite someone to a hayride. I really wanted to invite this cute, shy guy who appeared somewhat removed but seemed smart and interesting. I was so nervous, afraid he'd say 'No.' I called and he said 'Sure, I'd like to.' I was flabbergasted. I had the most fabulous evening. It took nerve, but I learned from then on to take the risk."

Being Asked Out

How do you react if you're the one on the receiving end of an invitation? Well, the basic rule in this and all things is to be as honest as possible. You have several options:

- ✧ You may want to accept and do.
- ✧ You may want to accept but can't.
- ✧ You may not want to accept but do.
- ✧ You may not want to accept and don't.
- ✧ You don't know what you want to do.

Your first decision is whether you want to go out with this person. Do you want to find out more about him or her and have him or her learn more about you? The second decision is whether you can actually agree to a date: Are you free to go out because you're not dating anyone else and have no previous commitments? Do you feel your parents or your friends will disapprove of him or her?

Being honest, however, does not mean being brutally frank. You can say "no" without giving an explanation. On the other hand, telling him or her that you're involved with someone else might help him or her walk away knowing that it wasn't anything personal.

Also, don't try to be kind and ask him or her to call you another time if you really aren't interested. And don't feel obligated out of "honesty" to tell someone that the reason you are saying no is because they are boring or not good-looking. It is enough to say "no" and to cite a vague reason why it would not be possible for you at this time. Everyone understands a "no" from time to time. You've been there, too; if you haven't, you will be. If you really don't know whether to accept, don't leave someone hanging. He or she might want to look elsewhere if you can't decide.

Your level of enthusiasm in accepting or declining may signal a lot to the person asking. An energetic "Oh yes!" is interpreted as your having great interest and delight in being asked out by this person. You may not need to say anything more to get the point across that you accept with great pleasure. However, even if you decline, be polite; you are dealing with another person who was hoping that you would favor them, and they may have a good deal of emotional investment in this. At the very least, he or she has feelings, and no one enjoys rejection.

The Least You Need to Know

✧ A date is an opportunity to get to know someone better.

✧ There are many reasons why you ask a particular person out—some may be mysterious, even to you!

✧ Some simple conversation skills are all you need to ask someone out.

✧ It's important to be honest and polite when you respond to someone who asks you out.

Chapter 6

The Varieties of Dates

In This Chapter

✧ It's all an adventure

✧ The best way to control your expectations

✧ All dates are not the same

✧ Those special dates

So you've made it through the first step—you've asked someone out and he or she has accepted. You've successfully maneuvered through the first play of the dating game. Dating has entered your life.

In this chapter, I'll help you prepare for your first date by taking stock of your expectations. Then we'll explore the wide variety of dating styles, including traditional one-on-one dates and group dating. Let's get started.

Dating in the Twenty-First Century

In many ways, dating has been the same throughout history. At its heart, it involves two people interested in spending time together and getting to know each other better. In the past, during your great-grandparents' generation, young couples were always chaperoned by a responsible adult. Today, rules are more relaxed for most young people, many of whom are starting to date in their early teens. However, one of the most popular dating situations, as we'll see later in the chapter, is the group date. This dating style involves lots of kids going out together, some paired in twos and some on their own, all going to one event, like a movie, a dance, or a sporting event.

No matter what kind of date you go on, however, you're bound to be a little nervous, especially when you first get in the game. This is simply because you don't know what to really expect from a date, or, quite frequently, what you expect is not realistic or is very different from your date's own expectations. Indeed, there are probably as many different ways to think about dating as there are people who date.

Instant Replay

Katie, a 16-year-old, was so excited that Jeff asked her out. He seemed to her to be the perfect boy, and she felt convinced that the fact that he asked her out meant that he wanted to get involved with her. However, Jeff simply wanted to go to the movies and didn't want to go alone; Katie was a nice enough person and seemed to be fun. He didn't want to become romantically involved. Their expectations of what their date meant weren't at all the same. Although they had a good time, Katie was hurt. This was a case of unmatched expectations.

What Do You Expect?

Everyone going on a date has certain expectations about the event and about the person involved. Will going out with someone automatically lead to true love? Probably not. Is a date just a chance to have a little fun and get to know someone a little better? That's probably a lot closer to the truth.

The best way to approach a date is to take it for exactly what it is: an appointment to spend some time with someone you want to get to know better, preferably doing something you both enjoy. Dating means establishing a relationship, one that may or may not become romantic and close sometime in the future. Indeed, think small when it comes to casual dating. You're just trying to get to know someone you think you might like just a little better. Put aside—as much as possible—your fantasies of being with the perfect guy or perfect girl every time you go out. That way, if something special does develop, you're pleasantly surprised, and if it doesn't, you aren't terribly disappointed.

For most people, however, a date signifies a strong interest that at least one party takes in the other. If both people feel the same attraction to the same degree at the same time, then it's a lovely surprise. But remember, chances are the two of you will probably be on different wavelengths, at least at first. You might ask someone out because you already know (or think) that you're just crazy about him or her. Your date might accept only because he or she is curious about you or because the date seems like a good idea in a general sense. Just remember that in a relationship, the two parties may be at different stages of their interest and even their pleasure in the date.

Who Pays?

Is a date an invitation, or isn't it? Does the guy always pay— or is this an insult to girls who can take care of themselves? Should the person who does the asking always pay, regardless of gender? Or, should whoever has the most cash available always offer to pay? In most cases, it's the person who asks who should pick up the check because he or she acts as the host. If you're the host, you should choose the setting of the date with care, keeping in mind your budget. If you can only manage to spend $20, a movie matinee, complete with popcorn and sodas, is within your range. If you don't have much cash at all, a picnic at the park or a trip to the museum might be just the ticket. And if you're the guest, you should be mindful of the cost of a date and not go overboard on your spending.

Take Rick and his date, for instance. Rick, an 18-year-old senior, took a new woman out on a date to a movie. They had a nice time and talked a good deal afterward. They stopped into a nice restaurant late at night for a snack. The woman proceeded to order the most expensive thing on the menu. He was convinced she was trying to take advantage of him and only had an interest in being treated royally. That was the end of the dating fun for Rick—and the end of their relationship.

If you're not sure who's supposed to pay for the date, here are a few tips:

❖ If you ask someone out, you're the host and you should expect to treat.

❖ If you're the host, plan activities within your budget.

❖ If you're being treated, ask your host what he or she would recommend at a particular restaurant and take your cue from his or her answer.

Does that mean if you're the host you alway   s h everything? Not necessarily. As long as you're honest about the situation ahead of time, it's perfectly all right for you to talk—in advance—about sharing expenses, especially if you're doing something on the pricey side, like going to a theater or concert event. And, if you're the one being treated, offering to contribute a little something to the date is not only kind, but also a sign that you respect your date and appreciate the effort he or she is making.

Dating: The Wide Varieties

As mentioned at the beginning of the chapter, there are all kinds of dating situations, each with its own set of dynamics and pros and cons. In the sections to follow, we will take a look at six types of dates: the couple's date, double-dating, the group date, party time, the "big dance," and the "hanging-out" date.

The Couple's Date

Two people going out alone to some kind of event—a dance, a movie, a meal, a walk in the park—is the most basic date of all. Being alone together certainly has its advantages as you try to get to know each other. You have fewer distractions, you can better control the mood and the environment, and you can more easily establish a sense of intimacy between you without others around. Indeed, if the purpose of a date is to deepen your knowledge about each other, a private date is probably the fastest way to meet your goal.

On the other hand, some people find that having other people around is the way to go, especially if their conversation skills leave something to be desired. Having others around also lets each of you see how the other interacts with other people, which is an important clue to how you'll get along in the long run. That's why choosing one of two other kinds of dates may be a better option.

The Double Date

Four people, usually two of them good friends, in two pairs, form the typical double date. The advantage of this kind of date is that at least two people (the friends) know each other pretty well, so a good mood is often set at the start. Also, some people find it easier to relax when the focus is more diverse. And when the four people all get along, the result can be a memorable occasion.

However, there are disadvantages as well, primarily that friendship between the two people may become the focal point of the evening, which can leave their dates feeling out of it. If you decide to double-date, make sure you pay at least as much, or perhaps even a little more, attention to your date as you do to the rest of the people with you.

Instant Replay

Steve and Mike, two 18-year-old good friends, decided to double-date. They each asked girls they liked. The problem was that they did not realize that the girls intensely disliked each other and were very competitive. What started as a good idea ended with each girl not relating at all to the other and feeling as if their dates had tried to "set them up" to have a bad time. This reflected badly on Steve and Mike.

The Group Date

A group date can be a lot of fun. Often there are pairs within the group, and often everyone in the group knows each other. The couples involved can relate to each other at given moments in the evening, but they also get the chance to experience the group dynamic. There are other people around to help you out of awkward situations (should any crop up). You are also able to see how you and your date react together, as a couple, to your friends and acquaintances. If you decide to go this route on your next date, you might feel as if you have the best of both worlds. You'll be with someone you really like and have a chance to get to know better, but you'll also be around a group of people having fun.

A group date is a fun, collective gathering of friends. In fact, it might remind you of the TV show *Friends:* The characters spend almost all of their time together, but they are constantly forming couples within that group, or with others they bring into the group.

There are, of course, some disadvantages to group dates. The primary one is that you both can be so distracted by others that you forget to spend quality time getting to know each other during the date. Another problem is that you won't feel as much in control of the date. You won't be able to decide on your own what happens next, where to go, or what to eat. Now, this lack of responsibility can be attractive, but be aware of the pitfalls ahead of time, especially if this is your first date with your new friend.

Penalty Flag

Beware of the pitfalls of the group date with relation to you and your own date! Gina and Jim, both 19, went on a date with eight people—two other couples and two singles. Gina didn't like the fact that the choice of movie was not exactly hers to make. There was a lot of voting and discussion about where to go for pizza afterward. There was concern about who was driving. Jim related to her, but he also related to his buddy and seemed to be worried that one of the single guys was not having a good time. Jim and Gina were really not alone: They were really on a joint date!

Party Time

Another typical date is a party. You call someone up and invite him or her to accompany you. You arrive with your date at this great gathering of many of your friends. This is actually a group date of the widest possible proportion.

Parties are actually a great opportunity to show a date a lot about you. Your date will get to know your circle of friends and observe how you interact with them. If you're also kind and attentive to him or her, you'll also demonstrate what a great guy or girl you really are. Make sure you take the time to introduce your date to others and to make sure he or she has what she wants to eat and drink and feels comfortable during the evening.

Penalty Flag

Don't leave your date behind at a party! Not only are you a guest yourself at this event, but you're also hosting your date, the one you asked especially to accompany you.

The Big Dance

A big dance is a big date—it sort of takes on a life of its own. The school often takes a lot of time to plan the event, and in the meantime, everybody will be talking about who's going with whom. The big dance was often a big occasion for parents as well, who recall these events with some nostalgia. Usually, too much significance is placed on a particular dance; a week later everyone has forgotten it, and a new big dance is right around the corner. But the rule here is to ask yourself: "How will I have the most fun?"

Almost certainly, you'll have the least fun if you stay home. Or, you at least take away any potential for having a good time at the dance. I know it's scary, but give yourself a chance to have some fun even if you aren't used to being in a situation like this one. You'll do fine if you go without a date, especially if asking someone to go would make the event even more intimidating to you. Going "stag," so to speak, is even more fun if you have friends who are also going without dates. Today, some groups of friends—males and females together—treat a big dance occasion as a big group date, which is a great alternative to the traditional couple's date.

Instant Replay

Jon, 16, accompanied Lila, also 16, a girl he had recently met at a cross-town tennis match, to a party given by his high school fraternity. Lila knew nobody there. When Jon arrived with her, he was mobbed by his fraternity brothers who tried to joke around with him. But Lila remembered Jon for "how sweet he was"—he never left her side. When he spoke to friends and their dates, he took Lila by the hand and brought her around with him. He introduced Lila to everyone and made her feel very special to be there with him. She really felt that, even though he was sur-rounded by his own friends, he was there with her and for her. She liked that!

Asking a date to the big dance requires a bit more prep time. A big dance usually requires special dress, which means you need time to pick out a wardrobe. You'll also need to work out other details, such as who'll drive you to and from the dance and who's going to pay for the tickets. So ask someone as far in advance as possible. Remember that this is an impor-tant occasion for some people—something some look forward to with great anticipation.

You can do it! If you're a guy afraid you'll be turned down, you should know what a 15-year-old boy told me recently.

He told me that it was really easy for him to get a date to the spring ball. To his surprise, he found many girls eager to be asked because this was an event they wanted to go to and were hoping someone would ask them. You, too, might be very surprised to find out how easy it is to find a great date, and think of how much fun you can have.

Nowadays, however, it is perfectly acceptable for girls to ask the guys out to a prom or other big date. If a girl wants to go, she should clearly get in there and ask someone out, as opposed to waiting for the guy to ask her. But there are some other "games" that people still play which throw back to the time when women simply didn't ask men out directly; rather, they set up a situation which would encourage the guy to do so. And the techniques of asking someone out are the same that we have discussed in Chapter 5, "Asking for a Date."

The prom is the biggest "big dance" event of them all. Parents may put a good deal of emphasis on the prom because it's often one of their fondest high school memories. At times they may be more into it than you are! But it is no more or less than a big dance that occurs at the end of high school. Going alone or deciding not to go does not confirm you as a social success or failure. It's not your final examination in popularity it's just another event. So go for the fun, whether you go with one special person or go solo.

Hanging-Out Dates

Does going over to a friend's house and hanging out with them constitute a full-fledged date? The answer is a resounding "yes!" Dating is two people being together, getting to know each other, and having fun in the process. Dating does not require anyone to spend money or find some clever way to entertain. In the old-fashioned days three generations ago, dating consisted of "courting" and "calling on" ladies at their homes. Nowadays it isn't restricted to ladies at home, but the same rules apply.

In fact, having a "home" date can be great. You can get some real insight into your date's personality, preferences, and tastes. It also allows you to learn about yourself and your date from that same interaction.

One of the objects of the date is to have a good time. It is important to try to arrange an activity that you think your partner will enjoy. Trying to please a date is an important task of the dater.

At times, what seems like a "date" may actually not be one in the traditional sense, but it can still be fun and even romantic. Take Laura's experience, for instance. She was a member of the swim team, so she asked the guy she was interested in to come to a swim meet and just be there for her while she swam. Since he was interested in sports anyway, it worked out really well. Study dates work, too, although they're not necessarily good for your schoolwork! Just being together with someone you like or working on something that otherwise might be a drag can be a lot of fun. You might interact a little less, especially if you're really studying, but just being together can be very comforting and relaxing.

Knowing What to Do

There is an endless list of things you can do on a date. Going to the beach, to a concert, to a party or dance, or to the movies are the most common and traditional kinds of dates, and they all seem more fun when you have someone with whom to share them. But there are things that each of you might like to do that you could not envision the other doing with you—and those are some of the most surprisingly great dates you can arrange. The real advantage in not overlooking these opportunities for a dating experience is that it allows your partner to see a distinctive side of you in action. Rather than just talking about who you are and what you like to do, you get to reveal yourself in that activity.

Instant Replay

Amanda, 17, asked if she could go to the prom with some of the other kids who were going "dateless." So Amanda, along with two couples and two other single kids, ended up renting a limousine, going to dinner, and going dancing together. This group date was terrific for everyone. Everyone danced together and laughed together—and everyone included everyone else.

The Least You Need to Know

✧ Dates take on lots of shapes and forms.

✧ Your expectations of a date may not always match those of your partner.

✧ A great way to date is to go to large gatherings, but don't forget to pay attention to the person you're with.

✧ A big date like a prom may require some special advance preparations.

✧ The person who does the asking acts as the host and should expect to plan the date as well as pay for it.

Chapter 7

The Date Begins

In This Chapter

✧ Remember why dating is a good thing

✧ Techniques for making conversation

✧ The importance of having a sense of humor

✧ Factors that make a date worthwhile

Sherlock Holmes used to wake his sidekick Dr. Watson in the middle of the night and ask him to accompany him on one of his adventures. At this point, Holmes had already received some introductory information about a case and was now ready to act. He used to say, "The game's afoot!" as he awakened Watson.

In your case, you've asked someone out or accepted someone's invitation. The dating game has begun and you're on the playing field. The game is now afoot. How do you act to make sure that the date is the most successful it can be? That's what I'll cover in this chapter.

Identify the Dating Basics

Because dating can be both nerve-wracking and, at times, tedious, it might help to remember exactly *why* dating is a good thing. As discussed in Chapter 2, "Everyone into the Game," there are several objectives to a date:

✧ To have fun

✧ To learn about someone else

✧ To allow him or her learn about you

✧ To learn about yourself and life

Don't worry: You won't be able to meet all of these objectives on every date. If you just have fun, you'll have made good use of your time. Or, if you simply get together for a more serious purpose—to talk about an important issue and get to know each other's thoughts and feelings about it—you're doing just fine, too. In any case, it's important to prepare for every date you have. As is true for any game, you need to suit up, have some plays in mind, and know how to adapt. But, unlike most sports activities, the goal of this game is to make both you and your date winners.

Learn the Fine Art of Communication

If you consider that the most important goal of dating is for two people to get to know each other better, then you can imagine how important good communication skills are to the enterprise. This usually means coming to the date with a feeling of ease, a good sense of humor, and a certain amount of grace and consideration. But while you are in the process or communicating, it is helpful to analyze the communication taking place. You need to be able to step back and look at what is happening, either in real-time or after the fact. This gives you insight into where you are and where you have been.

The first step in communication is to master the art of so-called "small talk"—what I refer to as "casual conversation."

Instant Replay

Jackie, a 16-year-old, really thought that Scott acted too competitive with her. He and she seemed to be running against each other for everything—best Latin grades and school vice president. She really thought he regarded himself as too cool and decided to teach him a lesson. She asked him out to break down his confidence and to poke holes in his male vanity. However, on the date, they began to really talk to each other as people, not rivals. She learned a lot about him, his life, and his hopes. Jackie also began to share a lot about herself. She originally set up the date as a confrontation and contest—one that she would win and he would lose. In the end, however, they began to like each other. This was a successful date: Both sides won.

Casual Conversation

Casual conversation is how most of us communicate every day. It is a great communication style to use when you are first getting to know someone. Topics of casual conversation run the gamut from the weather to class assignments to opinions about movies and music. As casual and easy as those subjects may seem, you might still feel a little tongue-tied around your date, especially if you're just getting into the game. Fortunately, there are several ways you can improve your casual conversational skills. First, recognize that most everyone finds conversation a bit awkward at times. If you're with a new, unfamiliar person or situation, you might find it particularly challenging. Chances are, your date feels the same way about the whole thing, and will work with you as best he or she can to make you both feel comfortable.

Second, planning ahead helps start any conversation and also keeps it going. If you know your date pretty well, you already have an idea of what he or she might like to talk about. If you don't, then hunt around a little for a topic that interests you both. Again, there are hundreds of categories from which to choose, including music, books, school, television shows, sports, news events, and hobbies, just to name a few.

To get started—which is often the hardest part—you could use the technique I described in Chapter 4, "Building a Relationship": the statement-question approach. You offer an opinion or make a statement, then ask your date what he or she thinks about what you've said. If he or she doesn't seem interested, move on to another subject in the same way—by making a statement and following it up with a question. Chances are, you'll get a good talk going sooner rather than later, especially if you take a few deep breaths and relax a little.

Penalty Flag

When you're trying to start a conversation, don't abandon a topic too quickly because you're nervous about how it's going. Stick with it for a while, so that each of you has a chance to express yourselves fully. Don't worry: You or your date will find a way to move on to the next topic when the time is right.

Let's study a scenario so you can see how a typical casual conversation might go between John and Mary on their first date at a local restaurant:

✧ **John:** I heard the best new CD on 98.6 FM today. It was the new album by the group The Rock Trio. (statement)

Do you like them? (question)

✧ **Mary:** I don't really know them. (statement)

What are they like? (question)

✧ **John:** Very much like the old Beatles my dad used to love. (statement)

Did your folks listen to The Beatles a lot? (question)

✧ **Mary:** All the time. My dad and mom even sing their songs at the table sometimes. (statement)

First, John sensed that Mary didn't have a lot to say about the group The Rock Trio, so he quickly moved on to another topic in the music category. She knew something about The Beatles, and then introduced the topic of her parents, which is something John could follow up on. Now, the conversation could take any of a number of directions: It could center on The Beatles, parents, or singing, just to name a few.

Let's examine another kind of conversation that doesn't involve the statement-question technique. In this scenario, Joyce engages Ron in lively dialogue:

✧ **Joyce:** Mrs. Jones is a very hard teacher. But she is one of those teachers who really stimulates you to work hard.

✧ **Ron:** I really think, in the long run, this type of teacher is the best kind. They really get you into the subject.

✧ **Joyce:** I didn't even like history until I took this course. Thanks to her, I'm really enjoying it.

✧ **Ron:** I love history. I really like imagining what life was like during the Civil War.

Notice that in this conversation, neither person asks questions of the other. Each statement elicits another statement connected to it. And each new statement offers other avenues for the conversation to travel. From a discussion of the teacher, Mrs. Jones, a conversation about the Civil War begins. From this point, the conversation can go down the Civil War path or back to the subject of history, teachers, or school.

Time Out

Always listen. The only way to converse successfully is to be aware of what your partner is saying and how he or she is saying it. Hear what your date introduces into the conversation, and let the focus of the conversation change and evolve as you continue your talk.

Joyce may have known ahead of time that Ron really likes to take challenging classes in school, and she began by approaching a subject she knew he'd enjoy. But, in the first scenario, John knew nothing about Mary's taste in music. So, when he began by talking about a musical group she didn't know, he had to quickly maneuver the conversation to a topic in which she had some knowledge and interest, The Beatles. Even if she didn't like The Beatles, she offered some commentary that allowed the conversation to drift into another subject: parents.

Directed Conversation

Directed conversation is a little different than casual conversation. You're much more focused on a specific topic and what your date feels about it, which helps you get to know each other well in a very specific way. If classical music is your passion and your partner detests anything but rock, it may be important to direct the conversation to that discussion topic sooner rather than later.

Topics appropriate for directed conversation are those that are most important to you, rather than the general topics you might choose for casual conversation. If you just adore watching *Felicity* on TV, you might want to draw out your date's opinion about the show. This way, you'll get to know how your date feels about something important to you. You'll also learn if you might have a date to watch the show the next time it's on!

Now that you've learned some of the ways to start and continue a conversation, let's take a look at one of the most important qualities to have on a date (or anywhere).

Laugh and the World Laughs with You

Ask anyone what he or she really appreciates in another person, and invariably you'll hear "a sense of humor." Not just the kind of humor that involves telling a joke, but one that allows you to see the humor in everyday events, to simply recognize the quirky, silly things that happen all the time. This means learning to relax a little and not take things too seriously. Indeed, it's essential not to get into the habit of taking dating, yourself, or your partner too seriously. View a date as just what it is—an opportunity to share some time with another person.

Again, you want to be entertaining, not an entertainer, so there's no need to take center stage at every turn. You don't need to tell jokes all the time in order to show someone that you see the lighter side of things. Just feel free to talk about things that you think are funny, like the time you accidentally poured salt into the lemonade instead of sugar, or the time your dog really did eat your homework. Human stuff like this, and your ability to laugh at yourself, can really endear you to others. Laughing at yourself and your situation also allows you to relax, and this does more to boost your chances of a successful date than almost anything else—except, perhaps, minding your manners!

Instant Replay

Janice, 14, was very excited about her ice cream date with
Marty. He was very good-looking, athletic, and smart.
Unfortunately, when they went to the ice cream parlor,
Marty ordered a double-scoop cone and proceeded to lick
it with great energy. It got all over his face, his clothes, and
the table. That was all that Janice could remember about
the date—that he was an unmannered slob!

Mind Your Manners

The word "manners" sounds so old-fashioned and stodgy,
doesn't it? But when it comes to dating—to any human
interaction—having good manners is essential. And having
good manners involves much more than chewing with your
mouth closed and using the right fork at dinner. Above all,
it means showing respect for other people through your actions, your words, and your demeanor.

Having consideration for others is a big part of good manners. Consideration means alerting your date to any change
in plans way ahead of time and being on time. If you're always late, it means you don't respect the value of the other
person's time because by being late, you're keeping him or
her waiting. It's true that plans change and delays are sometimes unavoidable. That's okay: Just call and let your date
know the change in schedule ahead of time, and you'll be
covered. Another thing you should keep in mind is that
you're both there because you've either extended or accepted
an invitation, which means that you're each either the host
or the guest. As discussed in Chapter 6, "The Varieties of
Dates," this means you must always put your date first. There

may be other friends of either of you around, and there may be other diversions. However, for this time you need to recognize that your obligation is to the person you're with.

Penalty Flag

Don't ever strand your date. It's never appropriate to leave your date alone—unless you've agreed to it ahead of time. As a rule, meet, greet, and hang out with other people together, as a couple.

Above all, consideration involves trying to do everything you can to make sure that both of you have had a good time. This means being friendly, open, and polite. Also remember to be gracious if you're the host and be appropriately thankful if you're the guest.

What to Do When the Date Is Done

As mentioned in Chapter 3, "Your Relationship with Relationships," one of the best ways to ensure that you have a better date the next time—with the same or different friend—is to learn from the one you've just been on. Now, this doesn't mean you should obsess over every word said or every event that occurred. What you want to review is the general flow of the date, the conversation, your feelings, and your date's reactions. Specifically, consider the following:

✧ **The conversational flow.** You might assess whether the conversation is working well, whether there is enough to talk about, and whether what you are talking about is interesting.

✧ **The general level of enjoyment and pleasure—both yours and your date's.** You might assess whether you are having fun and whether your date is as well, and why.

✧ **What went right and wrong about the date.** You might identify both the positives and negatives of the person and the date and what your feelings are about them.

Time Out

Keep a sense of humor and have fun, even when nothing works out—the movie is sold out, the restaurant has an hour wait, the car heater conks out, or you get a traffic ticket. Remember, having a sense of humor about these problems can help to make the date fun. You'll get to deal with the problems and laugh about them together. Sometimes these are the most memorable dates of all.

Remember: No matter how the date goes, you should be able to take away something of value—even if it's only the knowledge of what to do better next time. Did it work because you were able to laugh together? Or, maybe it didn't work so well because you talked for so long about your hobby—one that didn't interest your date. Too late, you realized that he or she started to get bored. Next time, though, you'll know when to quit. Remember that this is a first date, and the beginnings of a date may seem a little stilted. By the second date, the ice has been broken and you will be surprised by how much easier it all is. Of course, there's more to analyze than the level of enjoyment the date held—there's also the person you went out with. How did you feel about him or her? Did you feel that you had a lot in common and would like to see him or her again? You might not even be able to pinpoint what you liked about your date, but you know that you felt good about yourself and about the person you were with. When it comes to dating, that's the best result in the world!

It's good to analyze your feelings about the date. Did you each have different expectations about the date? Or did you monopolize the conversation so that your date couldn't get a word in edgewise? Maybe your interests were too different and you found little common ground. Although nothing can guarantee that you'll never have another bad date, the more you learn about what makes a good date good and a bad date bad, the better chance you'll have of creating more positive experiences in the future.

I hope you'll find some of the tips offered on the fine art of conversation useful. When it comes to assessing the level of enjoyment, you should keep in mind that it's in your power to affect that level if you feel it sinking. Most events are not set in stone: You can leave a party early if it is not enjoyable, and you can wander from one movie to another in the multiplex if the first film seems boring. Even if you can't alter the plan for one reason or another, keep in mind that often just being together is enough to make a date pleasurable. Indeed, even suffering through some awful experience can be fun if you're doing it with someone you like.

The Least You Need to Know

⬥ An important goal of the first date is to get to know the other person.

⬥ Conversation is a key to the development of this new relationship.

⬥ Good manners involve approaching others with politeness, humor, and consideration.

⬥ During your date, you need to be in touch with what's happening, question whether it's working, and evaluate whether you need to alter your actions.

Chapter 8

Keeping Things Going

In This Chapter

✧ Continuing the fun

✧ Making room for others

✧ Showing your feelings

✧ Concluding the date

The game is in play. The date is in progress. The two of you have met up and have started talking. You seem to like being with each other. You thought there might have been a bit of awkwardness when you first met, but soon you felt more relaxed, as if you were talking to any other friend. You're grateful that you took the time to come up with some discussion topics, but it turns out you didn't really need them. It all seems pretty natural. But that was just the beginning.

In this chapter, I'll give you some ideas for keeping the relationship going strong after that crucial first date, which means learning to deal with the outside world of parents, friends, and schoolmates. The fascinating part of dating is that dating is relating; through the process of dating, you're

moving forward a relationship. There is a very quick estab-
lishment of a relationship as you date: It is often concen-
trated, intense, and very rich.

Momentum: Setting the Date in Motion

In physics, there's an essential concept called "momentum,"
which involves the principle that when something is set in
motion, it stays in motion unless external forces stop it.
Something similar can happen in a relationship: You feel like
you're on automatic pilot, relaxing, enjoying the flight, and
moving along without any gray clouds or turbulence.

But that's when it can get dangerous. You've always got to be
alert to the internal or external forces that can put your dating relationship to an end. If you're flying in a plane, the
cockpit dashboard lights up with yellow and red warning
signs. In a dating relationship, the signs aren't as obvious,
but you still need to plan for these bumps in the road. Avoid-
ing them can allow your relationship to sail along smoothly.
Not heeding them can result in a strained relationship in
which the fun tends to diminish and the direction goes
astray.

Penalty Flag

Don't let the ins and outs of your relationship become the
sole topic of conversation. It's true that some people enjoy
talking about relationships more than others; and there will
be times when you'll need to discuss how things are going
and what you want in the future. However, a steady diet
of this may take away the thrill of just enjoying time together.

Do you know why most people date? Because it's fun! But, as we've discussed on more than one occasion, sometimes you have to plan a little bit in order to make sure both of you enjoy the date as much as possible. The more you plan, the greater your chances of having a successful date.

Time Out

Take it easy when you host a party. Not only will your guests have a better time if they see you relax, but you'll be able to enjoy yourself much more as well. Again, planning is the key here—make sure you have what you need on hand and then take it easy!

The first step is to choose an activity that both you and your date enjoy—or think you might enjoy. It's safer, of course, to pick something you know you like to do, such as go to the movies or to a sporting event. But it also can be fun to embark on an adventure into the unknown. If neither of you has ever been horseback riding, for instance, taking a supervised trail ride might be just the ticket.

No matter what you choose to do, the important thing is to try your best to have a good time and to show it! Fun is contagious, really, and if you let your date know that you're in a good mood and ready to enjoy yourself, you'll help him or her to get into the swing of things, too. And if either of you really aren't having a good time, then it's up to both of you to be flexible and adaptable and move on to another activity.

Including Friends in Your Date

When I talked about group dates in Chapter 6, "The Varieties of Dates," I mentioned that it's important for you and your date to focus primarily on each other—not your friends—during your time together. However, this can get tricky when friends are involved in the date—whether they're your friends or your date's friends.

Putting Your Date First

It's hard to resist the temptation to concentrate on chatting with your friends, especially if you're not so great at making conversation with a date one-on-one, but that's an absolute no-no when it comes to dating etiquette.

This isn't to say that interacting with your friends isn't allowed. Not only can including friends on a date add to the fun, it also allows your date to get to know you better by seeing the kinds of friends you choose and how you interact with them. As long as you include your date in your conversations and activities, you'll probably increase your chances of having a good time. However, there are some rules to follow if you include your friends on a date. First, it's crucial to introduce your date to the rest of the group—although your date may know some of the people, don't take that for granted. Second, make sure that your date feels welcome in your circle of friends. And third, always remember that you're with a date—this means never leaving him or her alone unless you're quite sure that he or she is comfortable and is being entertained.

Fitting In

Getting together with your partner's friends on a date can be very enjoyable. Not only will you find out what kind of people your date enjoys being with, you also get to see how your date interacts with others. You'll also learn whether—should your relationship continue—you'll like hanging out together with his or her friends. When you're on a date that includes your date's friends, try to be as open and friendly as possible. That will make your time more enjoyable, of course, but it will make your date feel good as well. After all, he or she invited his friends so that you could meet them, and no doubt wants you all to like each other. Putting your best foot forward and giving them all a chance is the polite, as well as the most enjoyable, thing to do. Furthermore, this situation allows your date to see how you interact with others, how easily you extend yourself to others, and how you'll get along with these specific people in the future.

Penalty Flag

When people remember and talk about the worst dates they've had, a common theme is that they were left by their date. This is not a couple in which one person dumped the other and ran off with someone else. This is a couple in which one person sort of wanders around alone, talks with others, and acts completely oblivious to the fact that he or she is with someone. Don't make this mistake! Everyone likes and recognizes it when their date pays attention to them. Every survey of teens suggests that the most common reason for dissatisfaction with a partner is the partner not really being there for the person—and this means "there" emotionally as well as physically.

It's important to both you and the person you're dating to create a balance between spending time together and maintaining your outside friendships. In fact, a common problem among couples is that one member wants to spend more "alone time" than the other does.

Remember that a couple is still two people—not a singular set of twins who do everything alike. Spending time alone for one is natural, and one person in a relationship may simply be more independent than the other. Although one party may feel "left out," they need to see this in the context of an individual's fundamental need to be alone at times. Just don't read more into it, and keep it all in perspective: Every request to be alone does not imply decreased desire to be with their partner. And they can use the time to do some things by themselves or with other friends as well.

Instant Replay

Max, 18, was very nervous. He was sure that Jen had invited him to her friend's party so that she could find out whether they approved or disapproved of him. He felt uncomfortable and on display. And, in a way, it was true. That's what happens when a new person comes into your life. Of course, Jen wanted people she liked to meet Max, and hopefully to like and approve of him. And he really wanted his friends to like Jen! Max just needs to be himself, understand that everyone wants to feel included and liked, and extend his friendship as openly as possible.

For people who have a large circle of friends and whose circle means a good deal to them, this may be a source of some conflict. But it's something you must work out if you are going to continue dating. In order to allow your relationship to evolve, you're going to have to extend yourself to your date's friends and vice versa. Furthermore, if you do sustain a relationship, you're going to have to extend yourself into each other's families as well.

Meeting the Parents

Is there anything more nerve-wracking than meeting a date's parents? They really can give you the once-over, can't they?! It's actually the "twice-over," with focused eyes and many questions, questions that can seem like a police interrogation! How can you best deal with this situation?

One way to take the pressure off is to think of your date's parents not as authority figures, but as older friends. They are, in a way, your date's "very special friends" and you need to display the same friendly attitude to them as you would to his or her other friends and acquaintances. Be polite and respectful, but there's usually no need to be reserved. Jump right in and offer information about yourself without waiting for them to ask all the questions. In addition, make sure you know what they expect in terms of curfew and other dating rules, and then show them respect by honoring those rules.

If you feel put off by their concern, try to put yourself in their shoes. They want to be sure their child is in responsible hands. Be straightforward with them. Pre-empting their concern helps them feel comfortable with you and will probably go a long way toward helping your date like and admire you.

And, here's something else to keep in mind when being friendly and polite to your date's parents: Treat your own folks with equal respect. Your parents are in the same situation as those of your date in that they worry about where you're going and when you'll be back. Make sure they are also informed about your plans. Being open and communicative with them will help them feel comfortable with you and your choices.

Wearing Your Heart on Your Sleeve

The dates are evolving and you've met the parents. It naturally happens that you begin to like this person. It is a simple question: How do you show someone that you like him or her?

Penalty Flag

Act your age when meeting your date's parents! You want to demonstrate that you are responsible by being friendly and polite. Set them at ease by announcing before they ask where you are going and when you will be back. But do not try to assume an over-mature attitude, as if you are very experienced and smooth. That may get parents to worry that their child is in too fast a crowd. And parents are concerned about their children's safety—it is the appropriate role of a parent. In today's society, it is still an expected role for a male to be responsible for his date's safety, but each party should always exercise caution for the other.

Well, you actually don't want to wear your heart on your sleeve. That old-fashioned expression means that every emotion you feel is readily apparent to the people around you. Although you don't want to go that far, if you're dating someone you really like, you certainly want to let him or her know your feelings. There are three ways of demonstrating that you like someone:

- ✦ Acting as if you like them
- ✦ Saying the right things
- ✦ Giving silent signals

Most people are able to pick up at least one of these techniques. Doing all three will make the message quite clear.

Acting as if you like someone means being respectful and considerate of that person. It means listening to what he or she has to say, being polite and courteous, and trying to please him or her. "Actions speak louder than words" goes another expression, one that's particularly apropos to this situation. On the other hand, saying the right things at the right time can sure help to make your feelings clear as well. That doesn't mean you have to declare your undying love, but you can either state your feelings directly: "I really like being with you," or through sincere compliments: "Your sense of humor is the greatest. No one makes me laugh harder than you do."

Finally, nonverbal communication also can be pretty powerful when it comes to getting the message of attraction across. I bet you can tell when someone is angry with you before he or she utters a single word, simply by looking at his or her facial expressions and body language. This is also true when it comes to recognizing feelings of affection. The person you're dating will get the idea that you like him or her if you're relaxed and at ease when you're together, you smile kindly when you gaze at them, and you touch them affectionately when you're conversing. If you also take the time to dress well and groom yourself with care before a date, your date will know that the time you spend together is important to you.

Recognizing the Signs of Attraction

When you take the time to analyze the date after it's over, look for the clues I described earlier to see if the attraction between you is mutual: by the way he or she acts, by what he or she says, and by the silent signals he or she gives to you.

Of course, it's not always clear when someone is showing you signs of attraction and when he or she is just being friendly. That takes some practice, and no doubt you'll misinterpret some signs as you go along. At the same time, don't always assume that someone can read your mind or that he or she is the only one who needs to express feelings and emotions. Let your date know how you feel by giving him or her the right vibes.

103

Time Out

Let your date know that you're thinking of him or her and have his or her best interests at heart. At some point, you might want to say outright: "I want you to know that I really like you." You have nothing to lose by expressing your feelings at the right time, in the right way.

If you're completely confused about how your date feels or where the relationship is going, just ask. You can ask either by revealing your feelings first ("I really enjoy being with you" or "I really like you") and then asking how he or she feels about you. Or, you can simply ask outright what your date thinks about what you've got going. Of course, you should try to gauge the genuineness of his or her response. Remember, it's often easy to confuse graciousness and politeness with enthusiasm.

Saying Good Night: The End of the Date

Depending on when your date takes place, its end may come at four o'clock in the afternoon or eleven o'clock at night. Regardless of what time it actually is, there is a moment at the end of every date when it is time to say good-bye. You say "good night" after the conclusion of every date, and it may be more significant with time. But, when it comes to a first date especially, this moment can at times take on special importance. It's the moment when both you and your date might express how you feel about how the date went, and how you feel about each other. It also is a time when you may discuss, or at least hint at, the possibility of going out on future dates together.

There are no hard-and-fast rules about how to say good night. At a minimum, of course you'll bid your partner good-bye—and if you haven't had a very good time or sense that there's no chemistry at all between the two of you, you may want to say nothing more than that. On the other hand, if you feel comfortable about the date, you might want to add a few words about how much fun you had as well as thank your date for being with you that afternoon or evening. If you're thinking you might like to see your date again, you should step right up to the plate and tell him or her that. I know it's scary, but no scarier than asking or being asked out the first time. If your date is less than enthusiastic, responding, "Why don't you call me and I'll see," simply back off and get yourself home.

If the response is enthusiastic, however, you may wish to solidify a time for a next date right then and there. The advantage of doing so is that it keeps the momentum going; there's no "wait and see" about it, which also reduces stress. If you have had a good date and are reluctant to part, an arrangement for a new date also keeps the magic alive so that it doesn't feel as if the date is actually ending.

You may wish, when you part, to demonstrate some sign of affection. This can range from a smile to a touch of the cheek, shake of the hand, hug, embrace, or kiss. It is sometimes awkward to know "how far to go" without seeming too forward or appearing too backward. This is the time to take your cue from your date. It can never hurt to take it easy and go slow; if you're both attracted to one another and are ready to make another date, there'll be plenty more time for affection in the future.

For most people, a kiss—even a casual, quick peck on the cheek—is still a mark of real affection and nothing to be taken lightly. Even if you don't regard a kiss as a particularly serious sign of affection, your date might. "A kiss is still a kiss" is a line from the song "As Time Goes By" from the movie *Casablanca*. So be prepared for the fact that a kiss *does* mean something to most people.

Time Out

Eye contact is key! So is a happy smile. When you're saying good night—and the date's been a good one—show your date how you feel using these visual cues. Does he or she respond with a smile or a sign that he or she might like to kiss or to hug? How do you feel about that? Saying good night is very much like a dance, and you need to feel the rhythm of it so you're both moving in the same direction at the same time. Don't worry if you feel awkward; that's par for the course.

The Least You Need to Know

✧ Assure that you and your date have a good time by being flexible and adapting to a different activity if the date as planned isn't going well.

✧ Never leave your date alone while you wander among your friends.

✧ Be open to meeting your date's friends and family.

✧ Be honest and up front about your feelings; if you really like a person you go out with, don't be afraid to let them know.

✧ Treat the moment you say good-bye as a time to evaluate your attraction to one another and your interest in a future date.

Chapter 9

Getting Serious

In This Chapter

✧ Signs of moving forward

✧ Romance blooms

✧ Going steady

✧ Conflicts

You have become comfortable asking someone out for a date. The date has actually gone fairly well. You ask this person out for another date. You talk, and you learn about them. They learn about you. You both like what you learn. You continue to go out together. In fact, you have actually begun to establish a special relationship with a special person. You feel as if you want the two of you to only date each other on an exclusive basis. It feels great and everything seems to be going splendidly. If this sounds like you, you've just entered the next round of the dating game. You've met someone you really like and he or she—remarkably it seems—likes you back. Now you want to learn how to keep things going in that forward momentum that has served you so well so far.

In this chapter, I discuss what can happen when a relationship becomes more intense, which means I'll also talk about commitment and how to resolve conflict.

Thinking About Getting Serious

When does a relationship evolve from a casual friendship into a more serious romantic involvement? Here are some signs that such an evolution is taking place:

- ✧ You want to date only this person.
- ✧ You want this person to date only you.
- ✧ You increasingly like and are captivated by this person.
- ✧ You really enjoy pleasing this person.

While these different elements might come into play separately, eventually all are present simultaneously. And when all are there, the relationship is serious.

The first sign that this relationship has turned a corner is that you want to date this special person exclusively and want him or her to feel the same. In addition, the whole process of dating becomes easier because you both know that you want to spend as much time together as possible. This person becomes more and more a part of your thoughts and you enjoy being in their company more than anyone else. This isn't to say that you won't ever have a tense moment or feel competitive about staying number one in each other's lives. It simply means that at the end of the day, you really want that special person to see you as special, and to date only you.

Now, having a serious relationship can mean different things to different ages. Thirteen-year-olds will express "seriousness" in a different way than 18-year-olds. Part of this might relate to the interests of younger and older teens' worlds. And serious might also relate to the length of time a relationship has been going on. A relationship that is regarded as "serious" for two weeks is not the same as one that has been going on for months.

Record Book

Songwriters throughout the years—including modern ones—have often chosen the theme of love to write about, perhaps because it's so mysterious. Do you know the exact reason you're so attracted to your special friend? Probably not. Maybe there's something about how he or she looks, laughs, or thinks. All you know is that your date captivates you. Although you might gain some insight by analyzing the situation, don't expect to ever figure it all out.

One thing you'll feel when you decide that you're in a serious relationship is how important it is to please the one you care for. And in pleasing them, you really see how much you make yourself happy. You actually see that one of your missions in life is to make someone else smile. And one of the purposes of going on a date is to create a pleasurable time for both of you.

"I'll Take Romance"

You know the lyrics from the theme song in the movie *Titanic*. It states quite beautifully that love never ceases and that "my heart will go on." There have always been images that define romance. Some of these symbols seem to be universal: roses, soft music, candles, warm summer nights, and a warm, cozy fire on a cold night. On the other hand, some things take on new meaning so that what seems to be ordinary to others might be the most romantic symbol for a particular couple.

Instant Replay

Nancy and Ted, both 17, had their first date at a very ordinary café where they both ordered root beer floats. Now, on their monthly anniversaries, they return to that same café to enjoy that same treat. Needless to say, not everyone would consider root beer floats to be very romantic, but for this couple, nothing could be sweeter!

Being "romantic" makes you feel a certain way. It creates in both of you a sense of entering into a world where only the two of you exist and the only activity that you want to participate in is making each other feel great.

Time Together

Spending time together is more than just the way you continue to build your relationship as it gets serious; it's also very enjoyable.

Many couples who have become serious just enjoy being in each other's company. They don't have to speak—they just have to be together. However, when many couples are together a lot, they often lose themselves. Although you enjoy being with a certain person, don't forget that you are still both individuals. Think of yourselves as three entities together: you, your date, and you together as a couple.

"Going Steadily"

There are two concepts of "going" together more than casually: going steady and going steadily.

Instant Replay

Mark and Julie, 16, used to study together most evenings. What was interesting was that they observed strict studying rules: no radios, televisions, CD players, or even conversation. They really studied and rarely interacted. They had great fun by simply being together.

Just this side of "going steady" is the concept of "going steadily." What this generally means is that a couple is seeing each other pretty much exclusively, although there may be variations. Going steadily can be defined by couples in a number of ways, but it generally means ...

✧ Dating almost or absolutely exclusively.

✧ No ground rules of the relationship yet accepted.

✧ No acknowledgement of couple-hood yet.

Although you and your date may see each other pretty exclusively, you've not yet made a solid commitment to each other. One of you—or even both of you—may be dating other people, at least on occasion. You may not be ready to have a relationship that could be defined as "going steadily," and you feel more comfortable remaining "single," even if you really know you enjoy your special date's company.

In some cases, though, even if you hold back a little, you may find yourself moving on to a more firm commitment when you decide to see only each other. Seeing each other exclusively is what has been referred to as "going steady" almost since the beginning of time!

Going Steady

Are you ready to go steady? Before you can decide that, the two of you need to define exactly what it means to both of you. Every person, and every couple, may define going steady in a slightly different way. At the core, however, is a common understanding that you have an exclusive dating relationship with one another and—most important—that everyone around you knows about it.

When you decide you are ready to go steady, at the very least you need to begin by telling your partner what you think it means. Does going steady to you mean simply an exclusive dating relationship, or does it imply always being together? Do you think it means that you and your date are obligated to spend all of your free time with each other, or is there room in your life for other friends? You may regard going steady as an occasion that's marked by a special celebration, a festive dinner, or a piece of jewelry. Or, you may regard going steady as a stepping-stone into a sexual relationship. Whatever your concept is, you need to clarify it with your potential steady.

At the same time, you must listen to what your partner thinks going steady means—and then decide if your ideas are similar enough for the relationship to work. And the only way to make sure of this is to talk openly about it. Difficulties arise when both parties enter into this serious stage in their relationship with different ground rules.

Keep in mind that going steady implies that you're a couple in the eyes of the world as well as in your own eyes. Different social groups think of going steady as meaning something a bit different, but a common denominator is that you are both off-limits to other potential partners. In some circles, going steady is almost sacred; however, in other circles it is something that two people who date do often and for only short bits of time with many changing partners.

Going steady should mean commitment: You want to be with each other, and you want to be with each other exclusively. It is obvious that you care about each other. But when you go steady, you want to announce to the world that you are together as a recognized couple. It almost sets up a boundary around you indicating that neither of you is available for another relationship nor wants another relationship. Along with this commitment is caring and consideration for the other and a desire to make each other happy. Going steady implies delight in being together and pleasure in the thought that you are a couple.

Penalty Flag

Don't suck the romance out of a relationship by talking every detail and defining every rule about it. Yes, it's important to set some ground rules and understand what each of you has in mind, but you'll improve your chances of having a happy, fun relationship if you let things take their natural course as much as possible.

Going steady for a 14-year-old may have a less intense course and a briefer time line. Younger teens may naturally have a desire to be more varied in their involvement and not desirous of being tied down to a single person for too long. Going steady for an 18-year-old may be much more serious and involve major decisions like college choices and summer plans. For older teens, going steady may actually be the prelude to eventual engagement, even if the engagement may be several years away.

Time Out

There are some very committed relationships that are never defined by the two parties as "going steady." This is usually because the relationship has just naturally evolved, and the concept of going steady doesn't exist in this couple's particular circle. Going steady may be fashionable for some, but for others, it just may not be a "cool" thing to do. Couples can certainly be going steady without declaring so, but it is always wisest to discuss together whether you are indeed a "steady" couple.

Coping with Conflict

In most great relationships, moments of conflict arise. Recognize this as inevitable, and know that it doesn't automatically mean that your relationship is in trouble. Actually, conflict is often healthy for a relationship. After all, you are two people trying to forge some common ground between you. There is naturally going to be some give-and-take between you. And the give-and-take may include some heated disagreements as you work to sort things out.

In addition, because you're still growing and changing, you won't always feel the same way about the world or about each other. And you wouldn't want to. It's healthy to mature and evolve, but it also may be difficult because it's not a thing you can control. You and your dating partner may develop at different rates, so one week your opinions are almost identical and the next you've grown apart. At some point, you may even decide that you've become too different to stay together.

But let's not get ahead of ourselves. I just want you to realize that at the beginning of a relationship—and especially when you've both decided that you like each other so much that you want to go steady—you may think that nothing could ever go wrong, that you'll always stay in that dreamy "everything is beautiful" stage. But it won't. You won't always agree, even about the easy stuff, like what movie to see or whether or not to go to the prom.

And, depending on your age, other more serious issues can interfere: If you're getting ready to go to college, you might argue about what your relationship will be like when you're each at a different school. If you're younger, you might wrangle over what friends to hang out with or how much time you need to spend on schoolwork compared with extracurricular activities. It won't always be easy to sort out these challenges, but if you really care about each other, you'll take the time to thoroughly talk them through.

Instant Replay

Stu, 16, always remembered the wonderful relationship he had with Betsy, also 16. They never argued or seemed to disagree about anything at any time. So, he was very surprised one day when Betsy told him she wanted to break up. What had bothered her was that Stu didn't really ever want to discuss anything difficult; he just sailed over things rather than confront a problem head-on. Sometimes he simply gave in, and sometimes he just bulldozed his way through. But he never could discuss issues important to Betsy and important to the growth and stability of their relationship—simply because he wanted to avoid conflict.

Getting Through Arguments

Believe it or not, learning how to argue is very important! However, doesn't winning an argument depend on who speaks louder and eventually gets their way? Not exactly.

Think of it this way: When you argue, you're each attempting to resolve a disagreement by getting your own point across. In order to resolve the disagreement, however, you both have to hear what the other is saying and treat that message with respect and fairness. At the end of the day, you have to be sure that ...

- ✧ Your viewpoints have been heard.
- ✧ You have heard your partner's views.
- ✧ You are open to compromise.
- ✧ You have come to a resolution.

You have to get the facts and your feelings out on the table in a manner that allows you each to hear what the other is saying. It won't work if you shout, stomp out the door, or sulk. Furthermore, you need to be open to a compromise. Now, at times this is not a 50-50 proposition. A compromise may well mean that you yield to your partner or he or she yields to you. If you can agree on this result, then nobody loses—you both win.

What's hard for most people—especially those new to dating—is to recognize the importance of making joint decisions. A simple example: If you really want to see one movie and your date wants to see another, you've got to talk it through fairly and decide how to resolve the disagreement. One week, it might mean you'll see your date's choice; the next, your movie is the one you pick. And at times, you'll chose to do something else altogether—something you both would enjoy without any questions asked.

Finally, it's important, whenever possible, to conclude your arguments. Allowing difficult situations to fester may undermine your relationship in the long run.

Penalty Flag

Don't seethe—release! It's very dangerous to blow up over an unfinished argument; it's better to resolve it through quiet discussion. Some people even snap at their partners or avoid speaking to them at all. Needless to say, you'll never get anywhere if you take this approach.

The Least You Need to Know

✧ Going steadily and going steady are progressions along the couple's course to greater commitment.

✧ When going steady or seeing each other on a fairly exclusive basis, both parties must agree on definitions and ground rules.

✧ Arguing—to some degree—is both very healthy and very normal in any relationship.

✧ Knowing what a commitment means to both you and your significant other is important before deciding to take this serious step in your relationship.

Chapter 10

Breaking Up
Is Hard to Do

In This Chapter

✦ Knowing the danger signs

✦ Being the "dumper" or the "dumpee"

✦ Moving forward

✦ Dating again

✦ Lessons learned

You have played the dating game and played it well. You've experienced what it's like to have a relationship move forward from an initial telephone call to a real dating situation in which you see each other fairly often. You've gained some confidence in your dating style and your ability to relate to members of the opposite sex. But now you fear that your dating relationship no longer satisfies you. You feel that it's best to end it, or perhaps you think your partner is moving in that direction. Don't despair! You'll probably end many relationships before you settle down with the right person. It's simply a part of life—and in this chapter, I'll help you get through this difficult part of dating with as little long-lasting pain as possible.

It Ain't Gonna Be Easy

Right from the start, it's important to accept that if you've been serious about someone, breaking up with them won't be easy. There's no sense in trying to minimize the pain and disappointment, if that's what you feel. After all, you were just recently a part of a couple, and you cared for and loved being with a very special person. Sometimes, you'll be able to continue a friendship even if you're no longer a couple. Or, perhaps you've hurt each other as you've moved forward, and being friends simply isn't possible. Either way, you're both likely to feel pretty lousy about the breakup, at least for a while.

Record Book

Psychologists tell us the most significant causes of stress are any big changes that come about: changing schools, moving, or going through your parents' divorce are just a few. You'll also experience stress if you break up with someone you've been seeing for any length of time. Even if the relationship grew sour, or even turned really bad, there is a natural tendency for people to miss what they had. Just be aware that feeling bad about this is natural.

How Does It End?

It's silly to say to you, "Nothing lasts forever." While that's certainly true, it's not likely to comfort you any at this difficult time in your life. However, in most cases—especially when you're in your teens—your dating relationships will have an end. And they will end in one of several ways, including ...

✧ You both want to re-classify the relationship as a friendship, or at least one far less serious.

✧ You alone want to dissolve it.

✧ Your partner alone wants to dissolve it.

✧ You both want to dissolve it.

✧ Others want you to dissolve it.

Each of these endings deserves some special consideration.

There are some relationships which just move along at too frenzied or serious a pace, which may make one or both of you uncomfortable. You may simply decide that you are too young to be so involved or that you do not wish to make a commitment at the present time. You may want to see other people, sometimes just to check out what you are missing!

Instant Replay

Peggy, 16, decided that she was just too serious with Paul. She was a bit confused because she really liked him, but she also wanted to sample what dating other guys might be like. She had an idea that another relationship might be more exciting. She and Paul decided to tone down their dating and to see other people. In Peggy's case, she discovered through dating other people what was most important to her in a guy, and Paul had it. They got back together and dated until they graduated from high school and went their separate ways.

This does not imply that, like Dorothy in the movie *The Wizard of Oz*, you need to run away and experience another place to realize that there's no place like home. The function of dating is to find out about who you are, and often this requires you to explore relationships with different people. However, there is a risk you must be willing to consider if you want to date others while thinking that the person you're with really might be "the one." That risk is that he or she could find someone else during this "off" period. You might find that if you decide you want to get back together when you're finished exploring, your date is no longer available.

Perhaps the most difficult situation is when the decision to break up or scale back the relationship is not mutual. When it's you who has made that decision, you face a difficult challenge in telling your date that you no longer want to see him or her in a dating relationship. However, it's not much easier when it's your partner who's come to that conclusion. The best situation is when you've both decided that things are over. While this may be "easier" than if only one of you decided to break the relationship off, it still can be difficult and painful.

Finally, there is the very problematic situation in which you are being pressured by others to break up, such as when you or your date's parents decide that you should no longer see each other. In this case, you have to assess the reasons for your decision carefully, and if you decide to break up, do so gently.

Before I give you tips on how to break up, however, it might help for you to learn how to recognize the possibility that the relationship is ending before it gets really ugly.

What Are the Danger Signs?

There are a few signs you can read that things are not going well. Some of these are subtle, and some are very straightforward if you look for them.

While some of these signs may seem obvious, you'll only see them if you continue to analyze your dates as they occur, and discuss with your partner how things are going from his or her perspective on a fairly regular basis. Asking yourself and each other lots of questions is the best way to go.

Some of the most significant signs include ...

- ❖ **You don't have much fun anymore.** One of the clearest signs a relationship is ending is if you're simply not having much fun on your dates anymore. Although it's not possible that every single time you're together will be thrilling, you still want to feel stimulated and happy most of the time you're together.

- ❖ **You don't look forward to your dates.** You may grow into a pattern of dating—when you expect to see each other every weekend night—but find you're not really looking forward to seeing him or her anymore. Is it because you find things too routine, or is it because you don't want to be with this person so often anymore?

- ❖ **You see things in your partner that you don't like.** I've already discussed the true value of dating: The chance it gives you to learn about another person while discovering more and more about yourself. Unfortunately, sometimes you'll learn things about your partner that change your mind about how compatible you are with him or her. As you delve further into his or her personality and values, you may discover that you're not as in sync with them as you once imagined.

- ❖ **You find you have grown apart, find the relationship stifling, or want to go out with other people.** In Chapter 9, "Getting Serious," I discussed how important it is to recognize that change and growth are normal; as you and your partner grow, you may grow apart. Face it: You're a different person now than you were even six months ago, and you'll be different six months from now. Chances are, you and your partner won't grow in the same way or at the same rate, so you can't expect to stay together in the same way forever.

You might have come to this decision quickly, or not so quickly if the relationship slowly eroded over time. At the end of the day, you may just feel that you have to work too hard to stay together. Or maybe as you grow, you need to feel a bit more independent to pursue new interests and new friendships, and thus begin to resent the relationship itself. If the relationship itself feels wrong, or like a burden, you should trust those feelings and make some changes. Isn't it better in the long run to be honest, break off the relationship, and move forward?

Instant Replay

Ron, age 18, had been going with Brenda for the last year in high school. They decided to go to different colleges and to break up during the summer before college so they could enjoy the college experience and not be tied down to a long-distance relationship. This was really Ron's idea, and Brenda was angry. Ron, too, realized that he was very upset and ridden with anxiety. They went back and forth in their feelings and started college still upset about separating. It took months before they felt confident the decision had been a good one. They needed to re-establish links with old friends and initiate new friendships, but were both surprised by how terrible they felt.

How Do You Stop Going Out?

If the time has come for you to change your dating relationship, you need to approach this with some care. Unless you have only gone out once or twice, you both may have some strong feelings about what the relationship has meant to you.

You've provided each other with friendship and affection.
You've offered companionship and trust. It isn't easy to leave
this behind, even if you're looking forward to the future.
There are differences between breaking up a casual relationship and breaking up a long, serious one. You may still
feel very hurt, especially if you were the person who was
"dumped." Breaking up after a few weeks may simply be the
norm for some teens, especially younger ones. The techniques for splitting up may be the same, but the degree of
pain may be directly proportional to the time you were involved.

Time Out

Remember, breaking up is a natural part of growing up.
You're likely to form relationships with lots of people
throughout your teens and into young adulthood. Some of
them will be serious and others very casual, but most of
them will end. (With luck, however, you'll stay friends with
some of your former dates.) I know it's painful, but you'll
get through it—I promise!

First, make sure that breaking up is really what you want to
do. One way to figure this out is to make a list of all the positives and negatives about the relationship, and then review
the tally. Maybe it's worth it to you to try to fix what isn't
working, or maybe your list will show you that it's time to
move on. Have there been too many bad feelings to patch
things up? Is your relationship going to require too much
focus, attention, and work? Or is it actually possible to repair
the relationship with some honest interaction or even help
from someone else?

Of course, you shouldn't try to make this decision all by yourself. Bring your partner in on it; talk through the problems and concerns you have with him or her, and make sure he or she understands where you're coming from. That way, should you decide to call it off, it won't come as a cold and impersonal surprise. Once you've talked it out, you then need to act, which may be a pretty tricky thing to do. Once you've broken up, you'll no longer have a ready date for every dance or Saturday night activity. You're on your own, at least until you find another person to date. It may have been your own idea, but you might find things lonesome, at least for a short while. However, in order to move forward and move on, you have to move! This means you have to have that talk—the one where you say good-bye as dating partners, and get through the next stage of your lives as friends or as acquaintances.

When You're the Dumped

One of these days, it's bound to happen: A person you're dating will turn around and dump you. It'll feel awful when it happens, but keep these four things in mind:

- ✧ This happens to everyone.
- ✧ You're going to feel rotten.
- ✧ You'll walk away having learned something.
- ✧ Move on sooner rather than later.

By far the most important lesson of the four is no matter what happens, you'll have learned something—probably many things—through this experience. You might learn that the person you've been dating isn't the person you thought he or she was. Or, you could discover things about yourself that are valuable: Your values, goals, and interests may come into sharp relief when you confront the end of an important relationship.

It's time to move on. Sulking and brooding over this serves no purpose other than to make you feel like a victim. Think of it this way: It was fun while it lasted, but now it's over, and I now know more about myself and what I want than I did before.

Penalty Flag

Look at the positive side of things. When a relationship ends—even when it's not your idea that it end—it doesn't have to be a completely negative experience. Learn from it—about you, about what someone else's expectations have been, and about what went wrong. But don't focus on blame; breaking up should never be about fault.

When You're the Dumper

Although it's always easier to be the one to make the decision to break up, it shouldn't be *that* much easier! Presumably, you cared very much for the person you dated, and no doubt you hate the thought of hurting his or her feelings.

Therefore, when it does come time to break up, you'll want to treat your soon-to-be ex with respect and care. In trying to be clear, you may need to be direct—but don't be insulting. Instead of saying, "I hate you for always being so bossy and overbearing," you might say, "I need someone who can treat me more as an equal, not someone who takes charge all the time." The point is the same, but the tone of the second message is more caring.

What Do You Do Now?

Once you've broken up, you have three choices:

- ✧ Continue to feel wounded.
- ✧ Gradually get back into the swing of things.
- ✧ Bounce right into dating again.

Most likely, you'll kind of do all three at once—as strange as that might sound. You'll feel kind of crummy about what happened, especially if you were the one dumped. It really depends on how serious your relationship was, how long it went on, and what the circumstances of your breakup were.

If you were involved seriously, you may need to feel bad for a while. Even if you were the one who initiated the breakup, you've actually sustained a loss, and, as with any loss, you'll probably go through a grieving process, which is quite healthy. Do keep in mind, though, that as tough as it is, it's something everyone experiences as a part of growing up and of learning about yourself and what you want for the future.

Penalty Flag

Don't neglect your body, mind, and spirit as you go through a difficult breakup. Staying healthy and connected to the world around you should be your ultimate goal. Don't ignore the fact that you have the right to feel bad and that some time must pass before you can put things into perspective. But feel the pain, and then leave it. Although you may never be able to separate yourself from these feelings completely, you need to move on.

So don't worry—you'll eventually reconnect with the world around you. You may even decide to get back into the swing of dating sooner rather than later, even if you haven't completely sorted out your feelings about your past relationship. That's perfectly okay, as long as you don't confuse your feelings about your ex—however complicated those feelings might be—with those for your new dating partners.

A word to the wise: It's always best never to speak ill of your ex. You owe no one any explanation, but, if pressed, just state that it was "just one of those things." Or, say it was a mutual decision with no hard feelings. It may help to re-member that most people know pretty much just what you're going through. In fact, you'll probably find it very helpful to hang around with your friends, who can help you gain some perspective. Remember that your family can also provide much support at this time; they also have been there.

You can, of course, rush right into the dating game once again. You got injured on the field, you went down for a few minutes, you got up on your feet, and you are ready to play again. If you feel you are ready, by all means proceed. And you begin the dating process just as before. Only this time, you have had the experience of the complete cycle of begin-ning, middle, and end. And you are better off for that experi-ence.

What Have You Learned?

I hope you've already guessed, after reading this book so far, what I'm going to ask you to do next. That's right! Learn from the experience of breaking up. As I've mentioned, every relationship provides you with a chance to get to know your-self a little better. You've learned what makes you happy, and unhappy, about being in a relationship. You've been able to view how another person sees and interacts with you. And now you know what it's like to say good-bye to a relationship—if not the person him- or herself.

Now it's important to take all that you've learned from being with this special person, leave the relationship behind, and bring that knowledge with you into relationships you have in the future. In the next part of the book, I'll explore some of the elements that go into a relationship and how they help determine your chances of success in the dating game.

Record Book

The ancient Romans cited as one of the gods' finest gifts the ability to "see ourselves as others see us." It's often hard to know exactly how we come across. We try to look at ourselves from afar and assess who we are. But here, in a dating relationship, you have the advantage of having another person close by whom you can observe interacting with you. You can see whether they laugh at your jokes, cringe at your ideas, or turn on to your looks. And the best of all lessons, in the long run, is for them to be able to talk to you about the good and the bad.

The Least You Need to Know

✧ Most relationships eventually conclude.

✧ It is wise to analyze your relationship to see where it is going and to look for danger signals.

✧ Breaking up requires some planning, care, and compassion.

✧ You may need some time to grieve the loss.

✧ Most people have been there before and can help you get through it.

✧ You can take what you've learned from both your relationship and your breakup and use it to help you have happy, healthy relationships in the future.

Part 3

Training for the Dating Game: Your Behavior Is You

Ben's been dating a few different girls for a while now, and it's been great. But at the same time, and through the process, Ben's been learning more and more about himself. He's a little confused about his identity and he doesn't always know why he acts the way he does sometimes.

In this part, I'll explore the major elements affecting behavior. I shall explore personal identity, values and passions, and then discuss emotions and decision-making, a major reflection on your behavior. I conclude with a chapter on parents, the most important people in your life.

Chapter 11

The Search for Your Identity

In This Chapter

✧ You and how you see yourself

✧ What you really see

✧ You as an individual

✧ You as a dating partner

You have now had some experience in the dating game. You are a player and have sampled what life on this playing field is all about. But, like any player who wishes to get better in a sport, you need to take time to examine your skills, evaluate your technique, and assess your strengths and weaknesses. In this chapter, I'll help you explore your identity—who you really are in the world of school, relationships, and love.

Being Up for the Game

How fit and prepared are you for continued play in this dating game you're in? Every sports figure needs to look at his or her attitude and approach to challenges, as well as his or her mental and physical strengths and capabilities. And every player needs to see how he or she can fit in and adapt to the rigors of the game the longer the game goes on.

Indeed, you're the most important factor in whether you succeed in the dating game. Success depends on your level of commitment, sense of devotion, and enthusiasm for the chase, together with the fun of dating. The good news, which you've probably already learned, is that there really is no need for anyone to lose in the dating game. Everyone can come out a winner as long as you play fairly and with a sense of humor and fun. Now, that's not to say that every date will be a great experience, or that every partner will think you're the dreamiest person to be around; but with the right attitude, the game can remain fun and exciting.

Penalty Flag

Don't lose yourself in the dating experience, but remember that you've got at least one other person involved: the person you're dating. There is an old Jewish proverb of Hillel that states: "If I am not for myself, then who will be for me? But if I am for myself alone, what am I?"

An important task when it comes to assessing your game-readiness is to look at how you come across and act in a social dating situation. In doing so, you'll want to explore the following themes:

- ✦ Your self-image
- ✦ Your values and your passions
- ✦ Your emotions

❖ Your decision-making style

❖ Your parents and their influence on your personality

Record Book

In the 1960s, psychoanalyst Erik Erikson wrote *Childhood and Society,* in which he discussed how humans all go through certain stages of identity. One important stage is separating from one's parents and family during adolescence. What he cites as important is that adolescents establish their own individual identities as different from their parents and that they develop intimate relationships with their own peers and not be isolated.

If you're like most teens, you're now looking at the outside world and trying to see how you fit in. Let's see who you really are and how you and others see you. From the role that you've played all along among your family, friends, teachers, and neighbors, you've developed an image of yourself as a person. Now, however, you've added to that identity having been a dating partner with other people. This role may bring out new and unfamiliar facets of your personality that you need to examine and explore.

Looking at Yourself in the Mirror

You do this every morning. Let's face it: Sometimes you look at yourself in the mirror several times an hour! The mirror may not always be your friend, but it's a constant companion and it helps you assess how you appear to yourself and others.

However, keep in mind that you're not always the most objective judge of what you look like. You may look in the mirror and see many imperfections, but that's because it's in your nature—in the nature of all of us—to be self-critical. It is said that you are your own worst critic, for most of the time you focus on the negatives. You don't look in the mirror and see any of the positive things that you project, which most other people readily notice. It is almost as if you cannot make a balanced or fair assessment of yourself—something you hope others will always do.

Who that image is looking back at you in the mirror is unique. You have your own distinctive individual features that are different from anyone else's. The media have their own images of what beauty is, but that is the media's image. It is very important to accept yourself and your own beauty, which is but a part of who you really are.

It's Not Just How You Look

Quite apart from reflecting your physical appearance, there are other things that the mirror can tell you. You see yourself, but so do others, and how you appear to yourself may well be how others perceive you. When you look in the mirror and see a put-together happy person, know that others pick up on that when they look at you as well.

People get a sense about you from the very first glimpse, and, even before you say a word, they form an impression that's hard to amend later. People often come away from a quick first meeting with a new person thinking that he or she "looks kind" or "appears perturbed" just by a visual glance. Sure, a smile or a scrunched-up face may be a telltale sign, but there are other clues as well. In fact, your body language—the way you walk, stand, hold your books, sit down—is very much a part of your public image. What you finally say may or may not confirm this initial impression of your mood and your personality.

Now when you take a look in the mirror, try to imagine what image and message your body language sends to the outside world. Is it one of self-confidence? Is it one of self-doubt? How does a person looking and projecting like you come across? Remember, people often judge you by the way you present yourself, not by your background, interests, or even conversation.

Later, when you're an adult looking for a job, you'll learn that displaying self-confidence at an interview is one of the most important elements when it comes to nailing the job. Before you answer the first question, the interviewer has already sized you up by your promptness, your clothing, and the way you shake hands, sit down, and hold yourself as you speak. The conversational part of the encounter, in which you answer questions, talk about yourself, hear from the interviewer, and ask your own questions, is surely a significant part of the interchange; but the interview has already begun the minute you walked in the door.

And, as surprising as it may seem, that's the way all new acquaintances first get to know you: from the outside in. So when you're assessing who you are to others, you have to take a look at how you look to others as well.

Know How Others See You

Looking in the mirror will certainly help you figure out how you appear to yourself, but it doesn't always tell you how others see you. In essence, you project yourself in five different ways:

- ✧ Your physical appearance
- ✧ Your attitude
- ✧ Your self-image
- ✧ Your manners and intelligence
- ✧ Your opinions and ways of offering them

As we've discussed, your appearance is more than your features and the clothes you wear. It's also about the level of self-confidence you display. Of course, it helps if you're not just acting confident but also truly feel that you're a good, strong, interesting person. But that's hardly an easy thing to do, especially when you first get out on that dating playing field.

So far, we've only discussed your outward appearance, but equally important to the image you present to others is how you sound when you finally open your mouth and speak. Not only does what you say matter, but so does how you say it. Indeed, how loud you speak, the tone you take, and your command of vocabulary and grammar say a good deal about you. When you speak your mind, the people around you really get a glimpse into not only what you think but also the way you think. That's why it's so important to choose with care what you choose to express about yourself—your hopes, your values, your interests, and your background is what ultimately will attract (or repel) new friends and relationships.

How do you know how others see you? One good way is to ask, which is just what old friends are for. When you ask someone to help you assess your image, I suggest making sure you choose a friend who isn't the least bit competitive with you. Otherwise, you might not get the most honest opinion. And once you get going, cover it all: Do your clothes help you project the image you're after? Is your conversational style attractive to others? Is there something you do that turns people off that you're just not aware of? Think of what you can learn by asking these questions of a trusted ally!

Like What You See

Do you want others to like you? The answer is, "Of course!" Then you simply need to like yourself.

Make no mistake about it: You're unique, and there's no one else like you in the world! Right now, take a look at your positive qualities for what they are: the valuable assets you bring to new and old relationships. Get those positive qualities out there and show others who you are! And take a few moments to savor who you are and recognize your "longcomings" instead of merely concentrating on the short side of things.

Time Out

Learn to like yourself for who you really are inside. Groucho Marx, the great comedian, once remarked that he would not want to be a member of a club that would accept him as a member! Although that's pretty funny, it also says a lot about what low self-esteem can mean. And, the fact is, if you don't like yourself very much, it's not likely that others will like you much either.

Knowing Your Role in the Family

By this time, you're probably pretty used to your role as a son, daughter, sister, or brother. In earlier years, you bopped around just trying to see how much fun you could have within the constraints of the family circle. You now have evolved into your own person, and therefore have formed different relationships with your family members.

For one thing, you're probably far more aware of your mom and dad as the individual adults they are. They have their own personalities, opinions, and faults. They also exist as a couple with a dating relationship all their own. You look to them as a model for the way couples interact, which isn't to say you always want to adopt the model they present, but you'll certainly be influenced by what you see in your parents. They represent the closest actors in an adult relationship.

Your siblings, formerly pesky and annoying, may still be pesky and annoying—may, in fact, *always* be pesky and annoying. But now, as you grow toward adulthood, you can appreciate their other qualities and their own maturing personalities as well.

139

Instant Replay

Monica, age 17, realized the truth of something she'd suspected all along: Her mom, who until just recently had seemed as if she came from another planet, had a great deal of valuable information and insight to share with her. As she got older, Monica learned to listen to her mother's stories about her own youth not as boring advice but as actual insights into her mother's personality. She could see all the things she and her mother had in common—as people, as women. Now, their experiences were far from identical, but the challenges of boys, relationships, and school were similar when her mother was her age. And Monica could see herself relating to her mother as a daughter who was going through similar issues but at different times. Mom was suddenly a more sympathetic and friendlier figure—even a true friend.

At the same time, you must understand that your family members also grew up seeing you in a certain way—a way that may not necessarily mesh with the way you see yourself today. As difficult as it may be, you need to talk to your siblings and your parents about who you are, and what you expect from yourself as an individual and as a member of the family.

Independence Day

Unfortunately, there will never be a day when you suddenly feel secure and independent. That's a process that takes a lifetime to conclude, with many twists and turns along the way.

Time Out

Everyone understands what independence means, but for each person there is often a discrete event which signifies the sense of independence. For Rick, 14, the key to his sense of independence was the ability to go downtown by himself and wander around. For Sue-Ann, it was the ability to decide completely alone what she was going to do on Saturday night and with whom. The common thread here, however, is that they both felt liberated from their usual approval system.

But you'll certainly have hints that you're coming into your own as you proceed through the teen years. Maybe you'll get a glimmer of it the first time you drive a car by yourself. Or maybe it's school that does it—that important transition from middle school, when your life had more structure, to high school, when you're responsible for making more decisions about what to study, when to study, and what activities in which to participate.

The bad news is that with freedom comes responsibility. Indeed, independence does not mean never having to answer to anyone again. In fact, it usually means having to learn to communicate more directly and clearly with more people—and more adults—than ever before.

Your job, in fact, is to demonstrate your independence by demonstrating your sense of responsibility. Simple things can do the trick. For instance, take the act of telling your parents, your date's parents, and your date exactly what time you'll be returning home. It takes very little to do this, but the rewards are huge. In one fell swoop, you've shown the parents re-spect, gotten pesky questions about your intentions out of the way, and impressed your date with your finesse.

Seeing Yourself as a Person

The basic rule here is to be yourself! Get in touch with your own interests and represent the things you love to do. Teens often view themselves the way their own families or friends see them, but this may be based on an outdated image. You are not in sixth grade anymore, but your friends from that time haven't gotten used to the older—and better—you. I re-member one 12-year-old girl who was literally afraid to spend too much time in the school bathroom for fear that while she was away from the classroom her best friend might dump her for a new best friend. She was still teased about this when she was in tenth grade!

A major objective here is to be honest and to see the whole picture of who you are. Don't leave it to others to judge who you are, and certainly don't depend on how you compete in every activity to determine your self-worth. Indeed, there are certain competitive sports, such as tennis, that emphasize where you rank in a group above everything else. Some schools place the same emphasis on class rank or grade point average. However, that's a dangerous way to develop a self-image. You're special and unique, and will never be only the sum of your accomplishments within the group who make up your peers.

Seeing Yourself as a Boyfriend or Girlfriend

You may quite enjoy the title of "boyfriend" or "girlfriend," and feel very proud when you're a partner in a relationship. You may even feel very mature to have an ongoing relation-ship. Some people may regard your being someone's boy-friend or girlfriend as a reflection that you are growing up and really becoming a man or woman.

But you must pause for a moment to ask yourself a few questions:

⬦ What do you envision when you think of yourself as being a boyfriend or girlfriend?

⬦ What do you expect from your partner?

⬦ What do you bring into the relationship?

You may see only that it is cool to think of yourself as a boyfriend or girlfriend. However, there are some other attributes that you need to talk to yourself about.

You may also wish to consider what you expect of your partner as they assume the role of your boyfriend or girlfriend. Are your expectations similar, or do you each think of the mutual roles differently?

Penalty Flag

Don't fall prey to the temptation of assuming that someone else will change, or the even more foolish assumption that you can change someone. All relationships change you in many ways by giving you new experiences and testing new skills. But your personality and behavior is you; what you see is often what you've got. It is very difficult, if not impossible, to change someone else. Many a marriage has been doomed because one party believes that there are some problems with the other, but that the first party can change them.

Finally, it is important to understand what you bring into the relationship. What you bring is your identity—who you are. It is not who you have been, or even who you are going to be, but who you are at the present time.

Be aware of your identity and feel proud of it. Remember that who you are is what has attracted someone to you in the first place and makes you someone special.

The Least You Need to Know

✧ Finding out who you are—to yourself and within your peer group and family—is an important task.

✧ Looking at yourself with some objectivity and considering how others see you is also important.

✧ Making adjustments may be necessary to your role in the family as you mature.

✧ Asserting your independence is an integral part of your identity.

Ethics
Acceptance
Maturity
Integrity
(Girls)

Chapter 12

Your Values and Passions

In This Chapter

✧ What your principles are

✧ Your progression to adulthood

✧ What your dreams are

✧ What it is like for you

In the last chapter, I discussed what identity is and how critical it is that you define your own identity for yourself. But there are several other components to who you are. It is not sufficient to see yourself only as a player with your own individual style and persona. You also need to be able to bring to your sense of identity the values you hold, the passions you have, the emotions you convey, and the decision-making process you embrace. All of these elements combine to give you and others the image of who you are.

In this chapter, I'll help you explore those aspects of yourself in several different ways, including by looking at the people in your life who you consider to be role models.

Choosing Your Role Models

Who are the people you most admire? Who do you imagine you'd like to emulate? For some of you, sports figures hold the most allure, for others politicians or actors, and for some it's parents or teachers. Everyone has role models; it is part of how you decide what kind of profession to pursue and what kind of life to lead. You can have both positive role models and negative role models. Negative role models are the people whose lives and qualities you hope to avoid having yourself. In either case, role models help you move forward in the right direction.

Think about why you chose a particular positive role model. Is the person attractive, cool, rich, sexy, or famous? Is the person a leader, a visionary, or simply a force to be reckoned with? It is good to think about the attributes of a person you admire and why you admire them. This gives you insight into what things you hold as desirable qualities to pursue in your own life's quests.

We all learn from the important figures in our lives. Role models serve not merely as inspiration but as benchmarks to enable us to match our own interests and dreams with someone already out there living them. They help us think about our own values and the values we want to emulate. They are active components to our thinking about what is really important to us—our principles.

Developing Principles

Principles. Ethics. Morals. Without question, these aspects of your personality are among the most important to examine. Here are three questions that, if you answer them honestly and with care, will help you do just that:

✦ What do you really believe in?

✦ What principles do you live by?

✦ Which of these principles is the most important to you?

Your belief system helps define how you look at the world. The principles you live by are part of who you are. Some principles are absolute and cannot be compromised, even when you deal with someone you're trying to please but who doesn't agree with you. As the character Tevye says in the movie *Fiddler on the Roof,* "you can bend only so far before you break."

Most people develop a definite set of principles and ethics in their teen years, but psychologists know that the process begins in early childhood, even infancy, as kids learn the difference between right and wrong from their parents. Part of the way you learn is by seeing what behavior receives rewards from adults, and what receives punishment. But you don't develop these impressions into the rules by which you want to live, and to which you want society to adhere, until you enter your teen years. Sociologist Erik Erikson termed the period in your life marking the transition between what you learn as a child and the principles you form in adulthood as adolescence.

You develop a set of ethics because you are part of a civilized society. While there are some principles that most people adopt ("thou shall not kill," "thou shall not steal," etc.), there are some that you must consider and decide for yourself. Some of these may include:

 ✧ Is a "little white lie" permissible at times?

 ✧ How much of yourself do you sacrifice for another?

 ✧ How honest do you have to be? If you mistakenly get too much change back in a transaction, for instance, do you return the overage?

Each one of us is confronted with questions like this quite often, and our answers to them define us and define our relationships with other people. In the end, most of us value being "decent" people and interacting with others who are also decent people. How you think about some of these issues and what you regard as important standards to which you hold yourself and others become a part of who you are and how you are perceived by others. It is also a part of how you look at the people in your life.

Time Out

Try to hold back judgment and accept people for who they are—weaknesses, mistakes, and all. On the other hand, if certain kinds of behavior are completely offensive to you—if you cannot bear people who lie often or who manipulate those around them—you have every right to avoid them. What you need to do is to strike a balance between what you can live with and what you can't. What areas can be comfortably gray and what areas are definitely black or white?

Achieving Maturity

Maturity implies having achieved a value system with which you're comfortable. What do you think about when you consider the concept of maturity? It's another one of those concepts that means different things to different people, and there isn't necessarily a right or wrong answer. Your notion of your own maturity is also a part of who you consider yourself to be, which also becomes important when it comes to forming a dating relationship with someone else.

It is significant to bring to a relationship a standard of what you regard as a grown-up, mature way of interaction. Your perception should include your own ideas, your own roles, and a thought about how both of your sets of expectations intersect.

Developing Responsibility

That word again: responsibility. Wouldn't it be great if you could get older and still have no responsibilities to think about? Unfortunately, that's not the way it works—ever. As I've stated more than once: With freedom comes responsibility, and by accepting responsibility, you increase your freedom and gain maturity. Some people still find it much easier to deny acceptance of responsibility for their actions, and place the blame on others if something goes wrong. Sometimes others do have something to do with things not working out well, but it is important to look at your own role in events.

Instant Replay

Mandy, 18, was really crazy about Todd, also 18. She found him to be a great guy, and felt that he really cared about her. However, there was one thing about Todd that drove her crazy: He seemed to want to be constantly taken care of! It was almost as if he expected Mandy to become a substitute mother. Todd relied on Mandy to make arrangements for dates, remind him about homework, pick out his clothes, and drive him around. While this was kind of charming at first, it soon became annoying. Mandy basically thought of Todd as very immature. However, Todd certainly thought of himself as mature; he actually saw no reason why being taken care of should be considered a sign of immaturity. They had different opinions about what being mature meant; and the trouble was that Mandy found Todd's different definition a source of tension.

When it comes to relationships, responsibility means many things. First and foremost, you have to decide what you think your responsibility is within a relationship. Are you responsible for …

- ✧ Making someone happy?
- ✧ Satisfying yourself?
- ✧ Always being honest?
- ✧ Generating trust?
- ✧ Following through?

And do you feel your partner is responsible for bringing the same things to the dating table in order for the relationship to work?

For many people, a factor they most highly regard in their partners is their ability to rely on them for presence and follow-through. They sense that their partners have incorporated a feeling of responsibility—not out of duty but out of a desire and even a delight to care about another person—such that they can be counted on.

Time Out

Take it easy! All the "tasks" of adolescence do not have to be hard or unpleasant. Try to see acting in a responsible manner as a positive thing; one that means you're growing up and becoming an adult. You'll also find that it makes everything in your life—dealing with teachers, parents, friends, and siblings—much easier. Just equate responsibility with being your own person. You need to acknowledge and accept the consequences of your own actions as a part of responsible activity.

Looking to the Future, but Living in the Present

The future looks bright, doesn't it? You've got your whole life ahead of you, and it's great to have big dreams of what it'll be like when you get there. But, in order to look into the future, you need to have some real understanding of where you are in the present. Before you get ahead of yourself, take a look at what your life is like now, and whether you'll be able to meet your future goals.

Feel Free to Dream

Ever since you can remember, you've been dreaming about your future—about going to your first day of school, making the soccer team in middle school, or attending the prom as a senior in high school. As you enter your teens, your dreams about the future include some goals you can start to plan to meet now—what college you might attend, what career path you might want to take, and who you might want to form a lifelong partnership with.

Instant Replay

Harry, a sophomore in high school, likes Wendy for many reasons. But for him, what's most important about Wendy is that she's someone he can rely on. "I know," he said, "that when I need someone to talk to or to help me with something, she is always willing to be there for me. I never have to worry if I am interrupting her stuff. It's as if I have become part of her stuff. I can count on her."

Why is it important to plan now? Well, consider the fact that several of our presidents knew they wanted to follow that dream when they were still in high school. It helped motivate them throughout college and their early careers. Derek Jeter, the great shortstop for the New York Yankees, dreamed not only of being a professional baseball player, but specifically of playing shortstop for the Yankees. He practiced and practiced in order to make that dream come true. That's often what dreams provide the most: drive, ambition, and direction.

Allowing yourself to dream—about being a rock star or a doctor or a teacher—helps you further define your personality. Although not all of your dreams will pan out, they do hold clues to your future. And when you're in a relationship with someone special and can reveal those dreams in a safe and supportive environment, your exploration can be even more fruitful.

Don't be afraid to dream, and don't be shy about talking about your dreams with others. Your dreams capture a part of what your passions are. Some of your talents are well-known: If you're already acknowledged for your artistic ability, you may naturally have a passion to be a clothes designer or a famous painter. But you might have other passions that you've kept to yourself, and it might be time to let others know your secret because it tells so much about who you are.

Reality Testing

On the other hand, if you want your dreams to come true, it's about time that you see how realistic they are. If you really have no talent in the fine arts, it's unlikely you'll grow up to be a world-famous sculptor or photographer. On the other hand, if you truly love the arts, you can channel that dream in a slightly different direction, to becoming an art historian or museum curator.

Reality testing gives you a balance between what you dream of being against who you really are. The end result is a fuller picture of you.

Instant Replay

Barry was a good all-around student, and everyone told him he could succeed in any career he chose. But what he always dreamed of doing was helping mankind by finding a cure for cancer and maybe winning a Nobel Prize. He knew that he might be competing with many scientists in a terrific game of chance and risk, but this was a part of who Barry was. He shared his dream with Noelle one day, as they were having a picnic under a tree in the park. She was amazed; she had never thought of Barry as wanting to devote his life to scientific research. It was at that time that she confessed to him that she always dreamed of becoming an actress on Broadway. They had known each other for some time, but in discussing their dreams they gained tremendous insight into who the other person really was.

Choosing a Direction

There is a wonderful old British movie from the 1940s titled *I Know Where I'm Going,* starring Wendy Hiller. She plays a young woman going to Scotland to meet her stuffy, prim, and boring husband-to-be; she is very sure of herself and knows just where she is going. She knows, that is, until she meets a young man on the train who turns her world upside down. This movie has a happy ending, and she finds true love forever.

You might know exactly where you are going, or at least have some notion of where you're heading; or you may not have a clue as to what is going on. It is perfectly fine for you not to know exactly where you will end up. You are heading off on a road, which is the most important thing. And the road will change before you reach your final destination. Just keep your sense of yourself clear as you travel so that you continue going in the right direction.

Time Out

Try it out before you choose it! Great chefs are stars today; but cooking in a restaurant—even as a celebrity chef—means hard work and long hours. Acting is a popular idea for many; but the odds of making it to the front ranks are long. And auditions, rehearsals, and performances are work! See if you can meet someone who's working in the profession that you dream about, and get a reality check!

Sharing and Privacy

As important as it is to share who you are with others—especially those you date—you still have a right to keep some things private. Not everything needs to be absolutely transparent. You might have *some* aspirations you'd rather not discuss with anyone—even someone you're seriously involved with.

Clearly, as a relationship becomes more serious, couples will want to share more and become less and less private. Indeed, one of the joys of being in a committed relationship is that you can share private thoughts and moments with someone whose love you can count on. However, your comfort level with sharing will be different with everyone, so you need to define what seems right for yourself and for your place in any particular relationship.

Knowing When It Feels Right

Summing up your values and your passions boils down to one main question: What things feel right to you? Listen to your instinct on these issues. Your values, ethics, hopes, and dreams form your very core. Sharing them with others, especially those special individuals with whom you have a dating relationship, helps you further define your values and your lifestyle.

The Least You Need to Know

✧ The values you hold and the passions you have are two significant elements that define who you are.

✧ A system of ethics by which you live usually sets in by the time you become a teenager.

✧ Your level of maturity, and its component of responsibility, are a part of your values.

✧ Dreaming is a way of getting in touch with your passions, which must be tested with reality.

✧ The decisions you make in your life can sometimes be overwhelming; always stay true to values, be honest with yourself, and ask yourself if it feels right.

Chapter 13

Dealing with Your Emotions

In This Chapter

✧ Your emotional life

✧ Emotions and your identity

✧ The varieties of emotions

✧ Handling your emotions

Do you ever feel lonely? Are you ever scared—really scared— by a horror movie? Are you excited by your birthday, happy about good grades, and sad when your brother goes off to college? These are your emotions, and, as you probably already know, they're not always stable. Some days you feel fabulous: The sky is blue, the birds are chirping, and everything is beautiful. The next day you feel dismal: The sky is gray, the dog is growling, and everything is awful.

Have you taken a psychology class in school yet? If you have, you probably found it fascinating, since it helps you explore the complete emotional spectrum. You discover that the roots of your human emotions belong in your early childhood, when you first learned to adapt (or fail to adapt) to the changing environment. Knowing how you and others adjust to certain things in your life is a helpful tool in figuring out how to move forward to develop new relationships. In this chapter, I'll explore with you how emotions contribute to who you are and what they may mean to your teen dating life.

Trust and Honesty: The Bedrock of Emotional Stability

Teenage emotions are generally changeable and volatile. Erik Erikson, a distinguished psychoanalyst, called the teen years the time of "identity versus confusion." Many different feelings and emotions emerge at this time. Sometimes they change suddenly, and sometimes they remain for a longer period of time. Often parents can't quite keep track of the swift changes; frequently teenagers respond by saying, "Nobody understands me!"

It is so important for all teens—both girls and boys—to be able to express their feelings. You need to be encouraged to show your feelings of joy, excitement, sadness, and fear. Your feelings conspire to make up who you are. You need to be able to talk about them, understand them, and learn about them. And you need to be able to see those feelings in others.

In order for you to be able to do that, you have to cultivate two qualities in yourself and in the people you care about. Those two qualities are honesty and trust. With them, a partnership is sound. Without them, a relationship is heading for trouble.

The Truth About Honesty

Honesty is a central quality of all personal and interpersonal interaction. How truthful you are with yourself and with everyone in your life is a cornerstone of your personality. Others will judge you by how honest you are and, in the end, you'll develop healthy self-esteem and maturity only if you can admit the truth to yourself.

Instant Replay

Laura, 15, was crazy about David, 14. David's mother was worried about David seeing someone older. They hid their relationship from their parents. One day after school, David and Laura came home to Laura's house and started to kiss and make out in her room. A half-hour later, Laura's father came up the stairs and David jumped into the closet. As her dad drew closer, he panicked that he was going to come into Laura's room and perhaps into the closet; David jumped out of the window onto the precipice and was about ready to climb onto the roof. It could have been a disaster, but David finally decided that he just needed to be honest and take the consequences. He came back into the room through the window, and they both marched out to meet the father.

Without honesty, you have nothing when it comes to developing meaningful relationships. If you can't tell the truth, then, first of all, no one will really get to know who you are inside. Second, you'll soon get a reputation for lacking integrity, and people will no longer trust you. And, as we'll see next, without trust, you're really sunk. People are beginning to look at you as an adult; but a significant element of adult decency is honesty. Think of how the world would work if everyone lied at will and no one had any concern about carrying out a job with integrity. And on an individual level, honesty is a distinctive component of your reputation and a valued quality for generating a positive image.

Penalty Flag

Temper your honesty with compassion. Being honest does not mean being brutally blunt! Always try to offer a compliment along with advice or a letdown. If you decide to break off a dating relationship with someone, make sure you tell him or her what you did like about the experience instead of just criticizing it.

The Key Element of Trust

Trust develops out of honesty—you simply can't have one without the other. When you and a friend or date trust one another, it means you've learned enough about each other to know that you'll always be honest about your feelings as well as your opinions and your activities. When you're dating, you certainly want to be around a person who will try to be there for you, has your best interests at heart, and always tries to come through for you. To have someone in your life you can trust is one of life's ultimate experiences. You can be yourself with him or her because you know that he or she respects and trusts you, too. Earned trust is very appealing. After you establish trust with someone else, it becomes something natural, something you don't have to think about. It becomes a fundamental, unspoken way that you interact.

But be careful, because the loss of trust is very difficult to recover. Because of its very importance, a mistake in trust shakes the very foundation of a relationship. In a way, of course, it's much easier to be honest and trustworthy than it is to lie and cheat; there's far less to keep track of when you only tell the truth.

Coping with Jealousy

Just when you thought dating and your first experiences with love and attraction were going to get easier to deal with, along comes the green-eyed monster called jealousy. You look at your date talking with another girl or guy and—without having a conscious thought about it—your heart starts to pound, your hands sweat, and you feel a combination of anger and disappointment. That's jealousy for you. It's an irrational emotion, and one that's more often destructive than helpful; and unless you're made of steel, you'll have to learn to cope with it sooner or later.

Instant Replay

Jan, 15, said: "Whenever I went to a dance with my boyfriend, I was so jealous if he even talked to another girl. I would simply think he was going to break up with me."

Students of human behavior from as long ago as biblical times have told us of the power of jealousy and of its dangers. It's almost as if this emotion was singled out for special consideration because of its potential for terrible consequences. Deep-seated in human nature, it is an incredible force that can both keep people together and tear them apart.

A little bit of jealousy may, at times and within reason, be good for a relationship. French novelist Marcel Proust took it a step further: He wrote in *Remembrance of Things Past* that jealousy is actually necessary in a love relationship. It challenges you to renew your commitment to another person and to reassert to them as well as to yourself that you find them singularly important to you and want you to be singularly important to them. Without question, you have to learn to trust the person you're dating, as well as respect his or her right to explore other relationships. Furthermore, it's important that he or she return that trust and respect to you. But that doesn't mean that a little jealousy doesn't help clarify your feelings about each other. Learning to deal with jealousy, which may spring from normal and natural impulses, is an important task. You need to pause and see what you really want. If you have an understanding of exclusivity with your partner and you want to get involved with someone else, you should be fair and open about it. If you are only interested in socializing with others but not really getting involved, be open about that. Your needs may have changed, and talking it over is crucial.

Dealing with Anger and Letting Go of Grudges

We all get angry at times. Some things are bound to upset us or rub us the wrong way. We might feel someone has taken advantage of us or wasted our time, to name just a couple of triggers.

Time Out

When you get angry with someone, open up and talk about it with him or her. People say the wrong things at times: We all speak without thinking on occasion, so it's silly to take it too personally. Or, we simply misunderstand the situation. That's why it's important to share the reasons for your anger with the person you most relate to it and get his or her side of the story before you let anger destroy your relationship.

You can deal with your anger in several ways:

✧ Hold it in and seethe

✧ Explode

✧ Resolve it

✧ Hold grudges

Let's take a look at each method and see its risks and benefits.

Don't Hold It In and Seethe

Just because you choose not to show your anger doesn't mean that the emotion no longer exists. In fact, the more you hold you're anger in, the greater the effect it can have on you and your relationship. You may boil over with dissatisfaction, with an inner hostility masked by an outward pleasantness. However, this is exceedingly unhealthy.

Make no mistake about it: When you hold anger in, you only end up angrier—so angry that it can change your outlook on life and on people. You also have little chance of getting over the situation and moving on. Seething serves no one—least of all, you. It causes you to exist with an underlying framework that is hostile.

Explode

Now, exploding in anger is never cool, but it may indeed be a way to get the anger out and get over it.

Time Out

Try this: Get the anger out when you're alone! Explode if you must, but do it in private; then resolve your anger with others more quietly, after you have shouted at yourself. Or, try writing to yourself.

There are several things you can do to recover from an un-intended outburst:

◈ Recognize that you have lost it and stop as soon as you realize what has happened. Don't continue the explosion just to finish getting your points across.

◈ Pause for a moment to collect yourself, count to five, and speak softly with face muscles relaxed.

◈ Apologize for the angry outburst, but offer the excuse that you felt very disturbed or heated by the moment because of how serious you took the issue.

◈ Reiterate your points calmly and allow others to respond.

◈ Decide on what will happen next before parting.

Resolve It

Resolving the situation that has caused you to become angry is clearly an important—and perhaps the very best—way to cope. Becoming angry, expressing that anger in a productive way, and resolving it will allow you to sustain relationships and help them to grow. Doing so shows others—and yourself, at times—what things anger you, and how you deal with the anger. All couples with good relationships have ways to work through anger and resentment. Just recognize that anger is a normal part of everyone's emotional life.

Hold Grudges

The last thing you can do with anger is to never resolve it, and then become bitter and resentful of the person who caused it. In fact, a grudge is another word for unresolved anger toward the person you think has wronged you. Even if you interact with this person pleasantly, it is superficial; you have anger toward this person and may be looking for the time when you can get even.

Record Book

The Hatfields and the McCoys are two families in the South who have been angry with each other for generations. There are stories about the legendary feud and grudges between these two large extended families who hate each other just because they belong to one clan or the other. But there is no clear understanding of what started these events 150 years ago in the first place! Actually, earlier this year a Hatfield married a McCoy (Remember Romeo and Juliet?), with much celebration all around from the younger generation, who were eager to get on with other things.

"Revenge is sweet!"—or is it? It occupies your thoughts, wastes your energy, consumes you—and for what? Call it done and get on with it. If you can put the situation into context and see that it really matters quite little in terms of the relationship as a whole, do it. If you're really hurt and need to change the relationship, or even end it, talk it over with the one who's hurt you and move on. But whatever you do, let the anger go.

Doing Away with Guilt

We all have a conscience—what psychologist Sigmund Freud defined as a "superego"—that gives us a moral sense. When we do something that goes against our superego, we are often filled with guilt. As a general rule, most humans don't want to hurt other people, so when we do, we feel guilty and disappointed in ourselves.

You'll know when you really have something to feel guilty about. If you're seeing someone else behind a steady date's back, you should feel bad about what you're doing, the feelings you're hurting, and the trust you're betraying. The only thing that will take that feeling away is confessing to your steady and either making changes in your relationship that allow you both to date others or reaffirming your commitment to each other. Above all, you owe it to yourself and your partner to be honest.

Penalty Flag

Don't be afraid to break up with someone if that's what your heart tells you to do. Yes, you'll feel guilty, and yes, your former steady may be hurt for a while. But not recognizing that the relationship isn't working would be a mistake, for guilt can simply become overpowering if not confronted and rectified.

Avoiding Obsession

Obsession is that total concentration on a specific subject or person, when everything else in the world looks pale and uninteresting in comparison. Some students become obsessed with one of their classes, others with extracurricular activities, and others with their girlfriends or boyfriends. Being obsessive is important in some settings: You want a surgeon who is consumed with all the details of your operation, for instance. But in other areas you need to allow others to help and permit things other than your relationship to matter to you as well. A love affair is sometimes called "the magnificent obsession."

Instant Replay

Stan, age 18, had a girlfriend who wouldn't let him continue his ongoing male friendships. He said: "It was so hard. I felt that I constantly had to choose between her and my guy friends. They began to feel that I was a 'sissy,' and yet she felt that I needed to set priorities and make her number one!"

Although true obsession is pretty rare, a common complaint among teens who date is possessiveness: One partner wants to spend more time together than does the other. Learning how to balance companionship with independence can be complicated at times. However, it's important that one partner not feel overwhelmed by the other's need for closeness. This is not an impossible situation to avoid—in fact, as long as you keep the lines of communication open, you'll probably be able to find a happy balance between wanting to be together and wanting to maintain some independence.

Getting a Handle on Anxiety

Anxiety and tension are common conditions, especially today when it seems that we've all got more to do each day, and the competition for everything from grades to dates seems particularly fierce. Anxiety is a part of life's labors. Sometimes it seems impossible for you to function effectively because you are too concerned about the present or future—worried that things will not go right. Some people experience moments of panic when they have to speak before an audience or go to a gathering in which they do not know anyone. Sometimes this anxiety can interfere with a teen's ability to ask someone out or to be on a date and have fun.

You can, however, learn to cope with these feelings in three different ways:

✧ Recognize that feeling a little anxious may actually help you rise to an important occasion, and is the way we all deal with life's "deadlines."

✧ Focus on what you can do now to reduce the anxiety. Depending on what the anxiety-producing event is, you can learn to start studying earlier for exams or decide to go "stag" to the dance.

✧ Consider getting help from a school counselor or doctor if your anxiety starts to prevent you from performing your normal activities on a regular basis.

Moodiness

With all of these emotions coursing through you, it probably doesn't surprise you that moodiness may be part of the picture as well. Mood swings are particularly common in teens, doctors think, because you're also having to cope with rapidly changing hormone levels throughout these years.

People come to expect certain behavior from you. They often characterize others as "upbeat," "down," or "pretty even." But what is confusing to people is when you are positive one minute and negative the next. When that happens, they simply don't know where they stand or what to expect from you.

If you perceive that you're a particularly volatile person mood-wise, either by noticing it yourself or someone telling you about it, see if you can figure out what triggers the mood changes. Do they come on suddenly? If you're a young girl, could your mood swings be related to the hormonal changes that come with your menstrual cycle? Is there a particular event or situation that sets you spinning? If you can locate a reason for your shifting moods, you might be able to either avoid the situation in the future or at least learn to cope with it better.

Handling Depression

Feeling "depressed" or just feeling "down" is common among teens and adults alike. Indeed, we've all been there, when everything seems just awful and nothing seems likely to change. Feeling low like this is not only common, but also perfectly natural, even if it continues for several days.

But there's another condition that doctors sometimes term "clinical depression" that is far more serious. With clinical depression, the low feelings persist for more than two weeks, and interfere with your ability to enjoy any part of life as well as prevent you from studying, hanging out with friends, or even getting out of bed.

Being aware of actual clinical depression in yourself or in others is crucial. Some of the warning signs of clinical depression may include ...

- ✦ Staying in a room alone for long periods.
- ✦ Not seeing friends.
- ✦ Complaining frequently of headaches, stomach aches, and other somatic issues.
- ✦ Losing your self-esteem.
- ✦ Problems dealing with sadness.
- ✦ Having poor concentration.
- ✦ Gaining or losing weight (or anorexia or bulimia).
- ✦ Being angry (sometimes an emotion to mask depression).

Not all of these signs have to be present, and they may be represented in varying degrees of intensity. It's important, however, for you to recognize these behaviors as danger signs, and to get help for yourself or others if you see them occurring. Your school counselor, pediatrician, or family physician is always a good first step to seeking help.

Looking at the World Through Cynical Eyes

Author Mark Twain once commented that when he was 13, he thought his father was "the dumbest man" he had ever met. However, he added that by the time he was 21, he was "surprised at how much the old man had learned!" Twain was cynical—doubting and negative—about his father's intelligence: He discounted his father's place in the world and did not value his opinion. Cynicism implies a questioning of reality and a criticism of anyone's ability to do something about it.

It is natural for young people to examine the world around them, see what's wrong with it, and decide that they want to change it. Motivation may first be rooted in cynicism, but cynicism alone amounts to very little. It may be fine to look at the present day and be cynical, but it's important to marshal that cynicism to promote action.

Cynical people are not always the most pleasant to be with because they are always putting down others' efforts. If this is a part of your identity, it is important to recognize that constant cynicism is offensive and not the makings of a sparkling date. It is usually part of a "down" mood.

Going for the Joy

Joy is an emotion impossible to hide. Sometimes teens experience a sense of marvelous emotional "aliveness." They look at the world unfolding before them as a place of wonder. They see their lives and relationships as the source of great joy. Go for the joy on a date. Be upbeat and help your date share in your excitement about the experience of the date and of life in general. It's fun to be young! Don't be afraid to show it!

The Least You Need to Know

✧ Your emotions are a part of your identity and reflect how you appear to others as a person.

✧ Honesty and trust are two qualities that are crucial to the success of a relationship.

✧ Teens may normally experience a range of emotions and a range of emotional swings.

✧ There are four ways to handle anger, all of which have their own sets of risks and benefits.

✧ You must learn to cope with emotions such as jealousy, guilt, obsession, and anxiety in order to grow and develop within and outside of your dating relationships.

✧ Clinical depression or anxiety may require some professional help.

Chapter 14

Making Decisions

In This Chapter

✧ The importance of studying how you make decisions

✧ Making decisions

✧ Living with your decisions

✧ Changing what you or others have decided

So far in this part of the book, you've learned a lot about what makes up your personality and your person. You've explored your identity, your values and passions, and your emotions. Now it's time to look at another aspect of who you are: your decision-making abilities.

In this chapter, I will first look at why decision-making is so significant an attribute. Next, I will look at the process of making those decisions and the variations in that process. We shall conclude with some consideration of how you stay on course with decisions you have made, but change the course when you need to.

Why Are Decisions Important?

All of us make several decisions during any given day. Indeed, you might be surprised at how many decisions you make in your daily life—from what to eat for breakfast, to who to say "hi" to in the halls, to where to sit on the bus.

And, believe it or not, each of these questions has its own subset of additional issues to consider. Take the question of who you're dressing to impress. Friends? Potential dates? Your parents? Yourself? Do you dress to create envy in others? Choices and decisions tell so much about you—not just your likes and dislikes, but how you come to like or dislike something.

If you're wearing clothes (that you secretly don't like very much) simply because they're currently hot and you want to fit in with the cool group at school, that decision says more about what's important to you than it does about your taste in clothes. Everything you do in your daily activities is really a series of choices, and those choices should tell you something about yourself as well as represent you to the world.

Instant Replay

Kathy, 15, was walking slowly in very high platform shoes. If you looked at her closely, you might have seen that she was wincing a little in pain each time she stepped down on her right foot. Although these shoes were really the cool thing these days, they were really uncomfortable getting used to. She actually hated these shoes. But how could Kathy admit to her friends that she was too klutzy to get the hang of this walking thing? She would sacrifice comfort for style any day.

Decisions give you insight into what you really think about things. They also give you an idea about what someone else thinks about himself or herself. We are the product of many small independent decisions that conspire together and create our image. Knowing how we engage in this process helps us to know what really motivates our actions and the actions of others.

How Do You Make Decisions?

There are several steps in the process of making decisions. Depending on the importance of the decision, we may spend more or less time on each stage. The steps for the process are the same, regardless of the complexity of the issue:

1. Gathering information
2. Processing facts
3. Forming conclusions
4. Making the decision

Let's take a look at these steps one by one.

Penalty Flag

Even when expressing yourself, be respectful. Wearing jeans at a formal wedding may make a statement that you don't approve of the dress code, but it may also indicate a lack of respect for or interest in other people's expectations. Some people wear ties to the theater out of respect for tradition; for some it is giving a nod of acknowledgement to the acting company that you think the performance, play, or company warrants "dress-up" mode.

Gathering Information

Decision-making begins with gathering information. You take in facts and other information, casting the net for information as widely or as narrowly as you choose. Of course, doing so involves making another decision: How much information do you really need to gather, and what kind would be best? It is not necessarily true that the more information you receive, the better your decision will be; more often, it's the kind of information that matters most.

The process of gathering information may be very informal, very rapid, and not very scientific. Say you want to determine what's going to become the next latest style. You don't have to go to the library to do market research, you just have to talk to your more-stylish friends, scan the hipper shops at the mall, and look at magazines to see what movie stars or musicians are wearing. So, depending on what you need to know, your fact-gathering quest may involve everything from book research to casual conversation.

Processing Facts

After you gather information, you can process all the facts. You'll probably need to discount some facts because they come from an out-of-date or questionable source. You'll know that others are wrong right off the bat. After sifting through the information, you are now ready to evaluate it.

At times, you may actually make a sheet and study the data closely; often you process these facts in your head. A cool sweater costs $69, which will be 5 weeks of allowance; the sweater will allow you "X" amount of coolness for "X" expenditure of savings, allowance, or extra work; is it worth that much? You may also consider the workmanship of the sweater—whether it will last, how easy it is to take care of, or if it will remain in style long enough to be worth its price. All of this processing may take place in seconds in your head as you see the garment in the store and decide whether or not to buy it.

Forming Conclusions

After putting all this together, you reach a conclusion. Some facts may point in one direction, but the facts may be weighted, so that some count more than others. You may care little about how well the sweater was made; you just have to have it because it looks so great on you. You come to a conclusion based on your analysis of the facts, but you understand that the analysis may be biased.

Making the Decision

After completing the first three steps, you are ready to make a final decision. In this case, your decision is to buy the sweater. In other instances, you may actually make a decision that runs counter to your carefully drawn conclusion. For instance, even though you decide you really want the sweater, you don't purchase it because your mother will be upset since she just bought you an expensive sweater last week. Other factors may weigh in with considerable power, and you may be forced—sometimes for political purposes—to come to a different decision.

Timing often influences decision-making. A couple who is off to college on opposite sides of the country may conclude that they will break up before heading off in the fall. While breaking up may be the ultimate decision, there has to be an intermediate decision of when to do so. One party may wish to get used to disengagement from the other well before they go off to school.

You make a final decision by carefully weighing all the facts and then formulating your conclusion. A decision needs to be supported by the facts, consistent with timing, and attentive to consequences and pressures. But it is important to make a decision that feels "right" to you. Facts may lead you to one conclusion, but, if that conclusion doesn't feel good to you, it is probably not the correct one.

After you make your final decision, ask yourself: What weights did you put on certain facts in coming to a conclusion? What additional factors went through your mind in making your final decision? How do you approach this issue differently than your friends, or your dating partner, or someone else? You need to pause and look at how you process, how you reach your conclusions, and how you eventually make a decision. By doing so, you'll gain insight into your thought processes as well as consider what factors are more important to you than others.

Can You Live with Your Decisions?

After you have made your decisions, can you live with them? You'll feel great about some decisions, and not so great about others. You may think you know which will be which in advance, but there might be a few surprises.

The two most important considerations in living with a decision are ...

✧ Recognizing that decisions are agreements.

✧ Learning to adapt.

Instant Replay

Andy, age 16, felt as if the joke was really on him. He said: "It was my idea to break up with Holly in the first place. I wanted to see other girls, especially Serena. But Serena and I didn't really get along all that well. And Holly started going out with Ted, who is on the football team, and she seems to be really happy. It was really a stupid decision on my part to have broken up. I guess I just wanted to see what another girl besides Holly had to offer. Now I guess I can't get her back. I'll have to live with this decision, but it is hard to do!"

Decisions Are Agreements

The end result of all this decision making is an agreement or set of agreements that you now must live with. The way you'll work the results into your life will vary depending on the seriousness of the situation, the impact of the decision, and your general adaptability. Clearly, breaking up with someone you've been dating for a long time will be a tougher decision to live with than which outfit to wear to school.

Adaptability

The only thing you can count on is that your life will constantly change. Some people seem to roll with the punches a bit easier than others do—especially teens, whose lives seem to change right before their eyes on a daily basis. But there are some teens who do find it hard to adapt to change and really need more stability in order to thrive. Some people simply have some problem in adapting to new and unfamiliar situations and need to have a consistency on which to rely. Not having this seems to be unsettling, and adapting to new decisions may be difficult.

Time Out

Keep in mind that some decisions are irreversible. Choosing to have sex with a date is one of those decisions. When it comes to such serious choices, take your time. Think your options and their consequences through thoroughly.

Your ability to adapt to decisions gives you some insight into your ability to adapt to many new situations, including those that don't arise from your own decision-making processes.

You can also see how others react similarly. In some relationships, it is very important that two parties have the same adaptation skills; in others, it is fine if only one person is the primary adapter. The rule is simple—go with whatever works.

Can You Change Your Mind?

If the question is whether you can change your mind, the answer is unequivocally "yes." Humans constantly reassess their decisions in the light of new circumstances. Sometimes people make decisions based on good hunches, but sometimes they need to live with a decision for a while before they realize that their hunch was wrong. At times, it's impossible to know in advance exactly what the consequences of a particular decision might be. You may just have to test the waters to see if you want to swim there.

Penalty Flag

Don't think of a bad decision as a disaster. First of all, you can always learn from it: What made you make the bad decision in the first place—did you gather enough information and process it with care? Second, everybody makes mistakes, and so will you. Just pick yourself up, make the best of the situation you're in, and move on.

Of course, it's not always possible to reverse a decision and take the road you didn't travel—that road might be closed off to traffic now. If you decide to break up with your date and then change your mind, you won't necessarily be able to pick up where you left off. Your date may have found someone new, or may simply feel differently about you. This also happens when you take a new job, find out you don't like it, and then want to return to the old job. Sometimes you can, depending on the circumstances of your deciding to leave in the first place. But sometimes your old position is simply no longer there—someone else has filled it.

Everyone has felt at one point or another that he or she is at a "fork in the road." The fascinating thing about the proverbial fork in the road is that you may never know about the road not taken. You might have a choice between two new things, both of which might have some unknown quality; or, you might have a choice to do something new or remain where you are. You may at times fantasize that the other road would have led you to paradise, but that could be all in your imagination. Because you did not take it, you may never know for sure. Always remember, however, that just because the decision you made didn't turn out well doesn't mean that if you'd gone the other way, things would have turned out perfect. It may well have been worse!

Knowing how you make decisions—how you keep them or change them—helps you understand yourself better. You see what goes into your thoughts as you conclude that you want to rethink your original decision. You learn from having experienced the results of a less than satisfactory outcome to your decision-making processes. You see how adaptable you and others are. And you hopefully learn more about yourself and understand in what circumstances you might be able to do better in the future.

Time Out

Remember what led you to your decision if you start to regret it. You might have made it for very good reasons and it only turned out badly because of unforeseen circumstances. Let yourself off the hook, and move on!

The Least You Need to Know

- ✧ Life is a series of large and small decisions we make every day.

- ✧ Decision-making is an important part of who you are.

- ✧ Making a decision to change your life means learning to adapt to the consequences.

- ✧ It's not always possible to erase the effects of a decision, but you can always learn from every experience.

Chapter 15

Parents: Your Own and Your Date's

In This Chapter

✧ Dealing with rules

✧ Understanding parental concerns

✧ Dealing with problem areas

✧ Keeping lines of communication open

Ah, those pesky parental units. For most of your childhood, you probably either took their care and feeding of you for granted or—hopefully—you've taken time out to really appreciate the support they've provided you.

Now that you're a teenager, however, and searching for your independence, your relationships with all parents—yours, those of your friends, and, especially, those of the people you date—have become a bit tricky. It seems that every time you turn around, you have to prove yourself to one parent or another.

In addition, you're probably beginning to understand how important your parents and their influence on you are to the personality you've developed. And finally, you're realizing that the way you interact with parents tells the world a lot about who you are. In this chapter, I'll take a look at the role parents play in teenagers' lives. After looking at the rules they impose, I'll focus on some specific problem areas. I'll end by discussing some techniques for better communication between teens and parents.

Abiding by the Rules of the House

There is a wonderful song from the musical *Les Misérables* titled, "Master of the House," in which the innkeeper talks about his role as the person who sets the rules and norms of his inn for all his guests and employees, whom he regards as one big family. His big family is not necessarily a happy family, but there are rules to be observed and appropriate behavior to be displayed.

Time Out

Understand this: Your parents are not your roommates. No matter how democratic your family may be, the rules set by your parents are the ones you must obey—out of respect, love, and simply because they're the adults and you are the child.

Do your parents have rules? Most do. In fact, nearly every child throughout history has had to live under rules set by his or her parents. Take Jonathan, for instance. He's 17 and is really upset with his parents. "They simply don't trust me. I have to be home by 10 P.M. on school nights, by 11 P.M. on the weekends, and I have to finish my homework before I can turn on the television. I have to let them know where

I am at all times. I am turning 18 in eight months, but they treat me like a baby. These rules really bug me! "

Jonathan is expressing an exasperation universal to teenagers about the oppressiveness of parental rules. At the same time, although it may be hard to believe, Jonathan—and you—would feel equally frustrated if there were no rules at all.

Parents are parents, with all the rights and privileges that come with the job. You can't afford to offend them or wish them to be absent from your life. You may have heard the phrase, "I only mean the best for you!" too many times to count; but in reality, that's what's happening.

You may think you are at an awkward age at times, but so are your parents. They want to give you wings to fly, but don't know if you know how to land. They want to encourage some independence, but want you to demonstrate some re-sponsibility—often so that they can feel more relaxed about what they are allowing you to do. But they have the right to be concerned and the responsibility as parents to have cer-tain demands that concern your security, academic progress, and social maturation.

Before you go crazy over all your parents' rules, take a minute to think about them. Make a list of each rule you're supposed to obey, and then think about the reasons behind each one: Can you see what purpose your parents think it serves? If you really have a problem with either the rule itself or how your parents enforce it, it's time to have a calm and quiet discus-sion with them. The important thing is to look at rules not as a group of edicts but as discretely individual issues, each of which can merit discussion.

Why Rules Are Necessary

Your parents have rules for you to follow because they believe that following them will help keep you safe and the house-hold running smoothly. Despite what you think, parents rarely impose rules and regulations just to prove their power or to make you crazy. The safety issue is a real one: When they look at the world you live in, they see a scary one.

Drugs, irresponsible sexual activity, and even gang and criminal activity abound. Making sure you keep to a curfew, get your homework done, and meet your household responsibilities are ways that parents hope will instill in you a sense of self-esteem and self-worth, which in turn will help you avoid these undermining options.

Instant Replay

Kristen was 17 and really liked Bruce, who was 17, athletic, and a straight-A student. But she was very bothered by the way Bruce related to his parents. She liked Bruce's folks and was always pleased with the reception she got from them. Her concern related to their son: "I was really alarmed by Bruce's lack of respect for them. He is a great guy in all other ways, but I don't understand why he constantly puts them down for being stupid, for not being professional people, not knowing anything about the 'hip' things in the world, and constantly getting on his case because he doesn't like to do household chores. I began wondering what Bruce would be like as a husband if he treats his own parents, who obviously love him and are so proud of him, so badly!"

Another thing to keep in mind is that your parents were once your age, and it's possible that they're strict with you because they're trying to prevent you from making some of the same mistakes they made at your age. It might be difficult for you to think of them at your age or even being tempted to sample life in the same way as you are, but I guarantee you that they were there. Assuring parents that you're aware of their concerns should provide a great foundation for a discussion about the rules themselves.

Instant Replay

Miriam was 16 and angry with her mother for what she re-garded as a burdensome curfew policy. Her mother did not talk directly about her own life, but Miriam knew from talking to her grandmother that her mother had been a challenging teenager. She said: "My mom doesn't share a lot about her childhood, but my grandma told me that there were times when she was really worried about my mom. I do know she had a serious 19-year-old boyfriend when she was 16, and actually thought of maybe marrying him. I'm not exactly sure how sexually serious they were, but I think they were very involved. I think my mom was kinda wild! It's just that she thinks that by having me home by 10 o'clock will prevent me from getting too involved with my boyfriend. That can happen at eight!"

Discuss the Rules

When you sit down with your parents to talk about the rules you're having trouble living with, try to take each rule on its own. If it's an early curfew that's bugging you, talk about that one alone. Find out what your parents think is important to them about having you home at a specific time. Is it to en-sure your safety? or give you more time for your homework? After homing in on the real reason for the restriction, you may be able to come up with a compromise that meets both your needs.

Now Negotiate

The good news about rules is that whoever makes them can also change them when new circumstances crop up that warrant it. Your folks are aware that you are emerging into adulthood, and the measure of a true adult is responsibility. Show them that you are moving in the right direction and can be trusted, and you might be surprised at how flexible they prove to be. Try this: If it's your curfew that's bugging you, show your parents that you meet that curfew by returning home on time for several weeks. Keep up with your homework and strive to get good grades. After several months, talk to them about the progress you've made and the responsibility you've shown. Then, discuss whether you can loosen up on the curfew, maybe by adding a half-hour at a time to it. If they agree, don't abuse the new rule. Keep meeting that curfew until you've decided, together with your parents, that you can handle an even later one.

Learning the Rules of the Road

Driving has a special allure, probably because it brings with it such a sense of freedom. But with this freedom comes responsibility, and a great deal of it. Indeed, motor vehicle accidents are the leading cause of teenage deaths and injuries. Many states issue restricted licenses to teenagers, including setting specific hours when they can drive, and limiting the number of passengers they can have in the car at one time.

Parents are concerned with automobile safety. Although as a teen you have great reflexes and good eyesight, you also lack experience behind the wheel. In addition, you've got all kinds of temptations around you, to experiment with alcohol and drugs, to pay more attention to your date than to the road, to play with the radio instead of hanging on to the wheel. In addition, your parents may be concerned not only about your driving a car but also about you being a passenger in ones that your friends are driving—for all the same reasons.

While rules about driving may be a source of tremendous conflict between you and your parents, you shouldn't think of this situation as much different from any other boundaries they set for you. They make rules about driving for the same reasons they give you a curfew: to protect your safety and provide structure to the family. You can show them that they can loosen their restrictions a bit by respecting their concerns: Phone when you reach a destination, don't get parking or speeding tickets, and come home on time with the car gassed up and without a scratch on it. Do that for several months in a row, and you'd be surprised how much more they'll trust you.

In addition, make sure you choose with care who you allow to drive you around. As a passenger, you're very vulnerable to the skills of the driver. Never allow someone who's been drinking to drive you anywhere, or drive with someone who isn't an excellent driver. If you have to, call your parents for a ride; they'll respect you for your sense of maturity and responsibility far more if you do that instead of taking a risk.

Instant Replay

Laura, 16, said: "I know my parents are freaked because they are always afraid that I am going to be run over, get in a car crash, get kidnapped, or something. I just acknowledge that this is one of their concerns and address these issues straight on. I tell them who is driving and reassure them that she is a good driver. I always tell them who I will be with so they know I am not wandering around alone."

Just like with other rules, show parents your compliance with their rules on driving, document that you have done well, and then discuss whether some of these driving rules can be liberalized. Sometimes, parents may need to have some more stringent rules in operation earlier in your driving career just to be assured that things are okay. You will usually find driving rules can be changed the more you drive and the more you demonstrate your success in driving.

Complying with Curfews

We've already discussed curfews, but because they're the most common rules set by parents, they're worth another look. The safety factors motivating parental curfews are real. Parents do worry about their children's well-being, and might be especially concerned when you're out alone at night. The best plan is to go with the flow, demonstrate your willingness to be a big kid, and enter into periodic discussions about changing the curfew parameters—after you've proven that you can show your parents respect by being responsible.

It is important to pick your fights. You need to decide which issues you wish to discuss with your parents. As José, a 16-year-old, said: "For my parents, curfews are a big thing. I guess I have to comply. There are other things I know we are going to have some fights about down the line, and I don't want it to appear as if everything with me is met with resistance. I just think of my curfew as part of my daily schedule. I have to be at school at 7:45 A.M., at second period by 8:47 A.M., and at work at 4:00 P.M. Now I have to be at home by 8:00 P.M. on school nights. It's what I do every day, just like being on time for class."

Handling Criticism

Criticism goes both ways—parents criticizing teens and teens criticizing parents. This one is a bit tricky: You want to get your points across, but you need to do it in a respectful, constructive manner. No one likes to be verbally assaulted or told how bad he or she is. Criticism does not have to focus on the negative, but can show the positive side.

If you feel that your parents are always criticizing you, it's important that you discuss it with them. If you don't, you're liable to feel crummy about being misunderstood, which will only cause you to act out in ways that will engender more criticism and keep you from ever having a positive relationship with your parents.

Here are some tips to get you going:

- ✧ Acknowledge that there is reason for criticism, if you see that there is.
- ✧ Point out why you think things may have gone poorly.
- ✧ Emphasize what you think is going well.
- ✧ Ask for confirmation of those facts.

It's most important that both you and your parents learn to look at each other as people—people with feelings, good qualities, and faults. You might want to remind your parents of the good things you do every day; when they get busy and you've made more than a few mistakes (and you will!), they may lose a little perspective. Laura is 16 and has talked to her parents frankly regarding her concerns about their "over-protectiveness." However, she never approaches her parents with negativity. "I always start by telling them how I respect their parental authority and admire their concerns for my welfare—that I love them for being there like that for me. But I state how some of their practices don't give me the feeling that they trust me to be aware of safety and be a big girl. If I see some rule which I think is okay, like always calling even if I am going to be just a few minutes late, I tell them that— even go on to praise it. This way they get a taste of what I think is wrong along with what I think is right as well."

What if They Don't Like Your Partner?

Nothing seems to be more unfair than when you fall in love (or think you do) and your parents disapprove of the person you're with. No matter how hard you try to make them see your loved one's good points, they just can't manage it.

Sometimes, your parents have good reason to be wary, especially if your date has failed to show either you or them respect in the past. Or maybe there is something in your date's past or present that isn't right for you to be around. As difficult as that may be to believe, you owe it to your parents to listen to their concerns and make a balanced judgment about your safety and your future.

Other times, however, it's because they really don't take the time to get to know the person you're dating; they draw conclusions based on rumor or first impressions. Or maybe it's because they have formed their opinions based on your date's background or school achievement (or lack of it). If so, you have a chance to change their minds about the situation over time.

If your parents' objections to the person you're seeing truly are unfounded, you have to take the lead and show them that they're wrong. You do this first by listening—really listening—to their opinions. Then, as objectively and calmly as possible, you refute your parents' criticism and highlight your date's good points. Don't leave it at the fact that your date cares about you; focus on his other positive qualities. The important technique here is to take the bull by the horns and talk to them. You need to hear if they think your partner might lead you to activities of which they disapprove. You need to hear if they think you are getting too serious for the present. Part of maturity is talking frankly and being willing to share your views and to hear theirs. Then, slowly but steadily, and with you and your date showing respect and maturity every step of the way, you can work toward compromise and acceptance.

Developing Better Relationships with Your Parents

It is very important to spend some time developing your relationships with both your own and your partner's parents. It may take a small amount of effort, but it makes things go so much smoother. It may also wind up being surprisingly enjoyable.

How to Get Along

Your parents are very special people in your life. Although you can be friends with them at times, they can't be your true "buddies," at least not while you're still in your teen years. This is because they have to take a strong hand in guiding you through this complicated and challenging time of life. And—trust me—you wouldn't want it any other way.

Not only are they responsible for you, but they've got a lot of other stuff going on in their lives. They work, worry about paying the bills, and have their own relationships with friends and other family members. You need to learn to respect all that they do every day, especially because by now you've had plenty of experience with feeling overwhelmed and under-appreciated.

Record Book

Only one generation ago, it was the norm for everyone to gather around the dinner table when dad got home from work for a supper which mom had spent hours preparing in the afternoon. Nowadays, some semblance of a family dinner occurs only three times per week, and, with both parents working, school schedules expanded, and often only a single parent at home, you need to make special arrangements to have that important time together.

Ten Ways to Communicate

The following are the principles leading to good communication with parents:

✧ Take regular time to talk to your parents.

✧ Tell them about what is happening in your life.

- ❖ Ask them about what is happening in their lives.
- ❖ Talk about potential problem areas in advance.
- ❖ Take advantage of opportunities to tell them about the good things.
- ❖ Take advantage of opportunities to share with them evidence of your emerging responsibility.
- ❖ Recognize that your parents are overwhelmingly concerned about your welfare.
- ❖ Recognize that your parents were also once teenagers.
- ❖ Dream with them.
- ❖ Be yourself.

You need to be actively involved in seeking time to talk to your folks. Instead of making this a one-sided conversation, with you giving them just the bare facts of your existence, really talk about what's going on in your lives. As you grow and mature, you can act as a sounding board for your parents, offering them your opinion and advice when they ask for it. Tell them about some of the positive things that have happened to you and emphasize those situations where you demonstrated maturity and responsibility. Your parents do have your interests at heart, but it may be difficult for them to put themselves in your shoes.

Remind them that they were teenagers themselves, and talk about their own dilemmas at your age. Take the opportunity to dream with them about your hopes and plans for the future, and listen to them about their dreams. Just because they are older does not mean that they ever stop dreaming. In the end, be yourself and let them see you as an emerging adult individual. The rewards of communication success are that you and your parents can evolve into an adult relationship rooted in the closest family history; this is for most parents, and will be for you, a source of incredible pride and satisfaction.

And if you're dating someone on a steady basis, you'll also get to know his or her parents. You may be surprised at how close you may become to these people. In fact, if you break up, you may feel as if you've lost two other friends because you have to leave his or her parents as well. On the other hand, you and they may form a merely tolerant attitude toward one another; that's fine, too, as long as you both continue to show respect to one another.

It may not be essential to have as intense a relationship with them as with your own parents, but it is important to at least respect your date's relationship with them. He or she has been just as affected by his or her parents as you have by yours.

In the end, there is nothing magic about getting along with these special people: All you need to do is communicate. You need to take the time to talk to them about what is going on in your world and to understand what is going on in theirs.

Instant Replay

Patty, age 17, couldn't wait to call her friend. "Something happened today. I actually went out to dinner and had a real adult talk with my father. He shared some of the things that were really bothering him at work, and I told him about some of my anxieties about my boyfriend and school. It suddenly seemed as if we were talking together as people rather than as father and daughter. I really feel I understand him so much better as a person, and I think he understands me."

You have trained for the dating game by presenting yourself as a person with certain behaviors, which is important in letting others know who you are and in knowing who others are. Your behavior is rooted in the concept of your identity, your sense of values and passions, your emotions, your decision-making, and your special relationship with your parents. You are out there as a complete player and understand others who are playing the game. You are now ready for the advanced plays of love and sex.

The Least You Need to Know

✧ You have a very special relationship with your parents, one that has helped you develop your own unique personality and perspective.

✧ Parents have rules that you need to acknowledge and respect.

✧ Parents do care about your welfare, and negotiation about the rules must take that into account.

✧ It's crucial to keep an open dialogue with your parents.

✧ It will take some active effort on your part to get along with your parents or your partner's parents.

✧ The 10 steps to communication lead to immeasurable rewards.

Part 4

Advanced Plays: Love and Sex

Ben is now involved in a very serious relationship; he thinks he's fallen in love. But is it really love? And even if it is, does it mean that the two of them are ready for sex?

In this part, I'll explore what love is and how to stay in love. I'll talk about sexuality and sex, including how you can tell if you're ready for further intimacy, as well as how to protect yourself from the physical and emotional consequences of taking a relationship to that precious step.

Chapter 16

Falling in Love

In This Chapter

✧ Perspectives on love

✧ Varieties of love

✧ The meaning of love

✧ The power of love

✧ Love as an indication of you

As I've discussed, dating is a wonderful opportunity not only to get to know another person, but also to really get to know yourself. And that knowledge sure comes in handy as a dating relationship turns to matters of physical intimacy and true love. Love and sex are not the same thing, but they are, of course, related. You can certainly be in love and decide to re-frain from having a sexual relationship—and this is especially true the younger you are. Needless to say, both love and sex-ual expression are complicated issues that you should never take lightly.

In Chapter 18, "Sexuality and Sex," I'll discuss sexual relationships in more depth. For, now, I'll try to give you an overview of what being in love can mean to two people and to human dynamics in general. As you'll see—or perhaps have already experienced, being in love is both simple and complex.

What Are the Different Kinds of Love?

Love is an intensely personal experience. What love feels like and what it means differs from person to person, and even from relationship to relationship. Love is different with every person you experience it with.

How you define and experience loving relationships depends a great deal on your background and past experience, as well as the qualities the one you love brings to the relationship. Some young people equate love with romance—with flowers, candy, and moonlit strolls. This view of the experience usually comes from the movies and television, and though romance does have a role to play, being in love really involves so much more.

There are all kinds of love. First, there is a difference between "love" and "like." You know what I mean: Maybe you like vanilla, but you love chocolate—there's a difference in the level of intensity. In relationships, you may like many people without being in love with them. And it's even possible—but pretty rare—that you can love someone without really liking them much. He or she may be difficult to be around, and have lots of habits and opinions you dislike, but there's something about him or her that you find irresistible. You label what you feel for him or her as "love."

We can generally divide love into four main types:

✧ Crushes

✧ Puppy love

✧ First love

✧ Romantic love

Instant Replay

Jeremy was 17 and had been dating Sarah, also 17, for only 2 months. He was a "romantic" at heart: He loved to write poetry to her, bring her flowers, and talk to her about how beautiful the evening sky was. He realized one evening that he had really fallen in love with her. But Sarah was not pleased. Jeremy had become someone, she had decided, who was "in love with love." She saw him more enamored by the concept of being in love than being in love with her. For Sarah, being in love meant making a greater commitment to a person and all the hard work it takes to really get to know someone.

It's impossible to say which kind of love is more important or meaningful than another is—and there's no need to. A crush may be as absorbing and serious as a romantic love; and it may even last longer. Let's take a look.

Crushes

Almost everyone, at one time or another, develops a crush on another person. We most often think of crushes as strong attractions to people who are remote and unavailable, either someone you know (such as a teacher or the most popular kid at school) or someone you've never met (such as a movie star).

Crushes are great because they allow you to feel all of the wonderful swirl of emotions that come with love, but allow you to stay a step back from the trials and tribulations of a real relationship. Of course, you must also deal with the pain and longing that comes from unrequited love, but if you can look at it with a little bit of perspective, you can also enjoy the experience. It can also prepare you for what you'll feel like and want when a mutual relationship comes along. Sometimes dating relationships begin with a crush—you have met someone with whom you are intense about going out. You find this person unfamiliarly attractive; you may not even know why you have such strong feelings about them. Yet, you find this person occupying much of your thought. And this may be the catalyst for getting to know this person better, which means asking them out.

Instant Replay

Roger was a freshman in high school, and he recalled with great vividness the crush he had on his high school English teacher. It was true that she was a young teacher, but he was 14 and she was probably 23. It was widely known throughout the school that she had a serious boyfriend from college, but Roger felt undiminished. He found out where she lived, tried to talk to her between classes, and volunteered to help her during his free periods. He thought she was the most beautiful woman he had ever seen. He even was convinced that she most likely also re-turned his affection and assumed that her friendliness to him was evidence that she had similar affection for him. But he did see her one day happily walking hand-in-hand with her boyfriend, and he re-thought what it was all about.

Record Book

In the documentary *The Life and Times of Hank Green-berg,* about a great baseball hero, a woman confesses to having a lifelong crush on Hank Greenberg. It started when she was a teenager and he was a 24-year-old baseball player. The humorous fact is that she continued to have a crush on him throughout her adult married life; her children even brought her Hank Greenberg memorabilia for a scrapbook when she was in her 60s. Indeed, crushes occur at any age and stage of life.

Puppy Love

Puppy love is an endearing term for the first warm relationships that occur between young girls and boys. These relationships tend to be very innocent, but very close and tender. There is a feeling of delight in just being together and usually a desire to do so. Even though the term is called "puppy," this does at times evolve into a more serious relationship. Two people can be so emotionally involved that they can be very hurt when this type of relationship ends. Many adults remember several of their puppy love experiences quite well—they are so much a part of their important memories.

First Loves

Almost everyone remembers his or her first real love—even if they realize now that it wasn't "the real thing." But at the time it sure felt like it was, and it counts as such forever in your memory. Noah and Nancy were both 14 when they met. Nancy remembers how great it felt to be in love for the first time. She recalls, "It was fantastic. He would wait for me after my soccer game and his cross-country and we would walk back home together. Then, we would talk on the phone at night, and then we would meet for lunch the next day. He was the first boy I was in love with.

By it's very definition, a first love doesn't last forever. Other relationships follow until, if you're lucky, you find your true soul mate. But, a first love is no less important, despite its fleeting nature; in fact, not only does it allow you to "practice" being in love, it also provides you with some of the sweetest memories you'll ever know.

Instant Replay

Kathy met a boy at summer camp during the summer when she was 15. He was 16. They were counselors together, and danced and spent time off with each other at every opportunity. They listened to songs that became "theirs." They shared their deepest thoughts. He bought her a necklace and asked her to be his girlfriend. The intensity was overwhelming. They were in love. Unfortunately, the summer ended and they went their separate ways. Despite the end of their relationship, each of them felt that the "first love" experience they had was wonderful, and a good foundation for relationships later on.

Romantic Love

Also known as "the real thing," romantic love involves two people so drawn to each other that the rest of the world seems to fade into the background whenever they're together. Real love is a strong emotion that actually may cause physical reactions like a more rapid heartbeat and a kind of breathlessness. Various environmental elements help to create a background that fosters romance. Certainly, soft music, moonlight, and a star-studded sky generate a romantic mood; surely, flowers, dressing up, or being together at a memorable concert create the right ambiance. But romantic love is about what's in two people's hearts—two people who love each other's company more than anything else is.

One professor I once had referred to this phenomenon as "the genius of romantic love." By that he meant that an individual's personality, being, and environment can all be involved in creating and expressing the desire to be a couple. Man and woman evolved not just by mating but also by courting. One person charms another and is charmed in return!

Is It Love?

There is a marvelous song from the musical *Guys and Dolls* called "I'll Know," in which the heroine of the musical asserts that she will indeed know "when my love comes along." However, she is unable to describe how she will know. There is often a magical quality about love: You often can't describe what it is, but you know when you are there. And, when you are there, you feel different.

You have to have some trust in your own feelings. Chances are you're in love—or at least have a desperate crush on someone—if you …

- ❖ Think about that person very often, if not constantly.
- ❖ Want to be with him or her most of the time.
- ❖ Want to know more and more about him or her.
- ❖ Feel touched and fulfilled by his or her presence, as if he or she fills some special empty spot inside you.

For some people, there is almost a physiological response as well: Your heart may race, your palms may sweat, or you may feel light-headed. You probably won't be able to define what

it is about your love that makes you feel the way you do—
and the good news is that there's no reason to try.

Time Out

Learn to savor the experience of being in love and try not
to overanalyze it. Although it's important to keep tabs on
your emotions, don't neglect the joy of just savoring being
in love. Above all, experience it and enjoy! There will always be time to think about it as time goes on.

How much of true love is spontaneous and how much of it
do you learn as you go along? Most of us have been brought
up to believe that falling in love is a matter of luck. But in
the era of arranged marriages, young people were coupled together without ever having met, and hoped that they would
learn to love each other over time. In the play and movie
Fiddler on the Roof, one character, Tevye, asks Golda, his wife
of 25 years, "Do you love me?" And, in the sweetest moment
of the play, they both confess to one another that they've
grown to love each other in a deeply profound way. It was
the first time they'd said "I love you!" out loud.

And what about "love at first sight"? Well, true love—which
involves knowing one another in the deepest and most devoted way—never happens in an instant. It takes time and
commitment. But "attraction at first sight" certainly does
happen—two people can be drawn to each other in the most
profound way without saying a word to each other. If you're
lucky enough to have such an attraction happen to you, go
with it—but take the time to get to know the object of your
affection before doing anything rash.

What would one look for in a person to love? Qualities such as honesty, intelligence, compassion, and kindness are certainly right up there. You also want someone who listens to others, who is able to share his or her feelings, and who has the capacity to give and receive love.

Apart from those basic essentials, what you look for in someone to love depends completely on your own unique personality and interests. If you love going to the movies, it might be fun to have a love relationship who shares that interest. Or, opposites might attract: If you're particularly outgoing, it might interest you to date someone who is very quiet and reserved. What makes you fall in love is completely personal, unique to you and the one you love.

There are, however, some qualities to avoid—no matter how attracted you are to another person. Stay away from someone who …

- ✧ Has a dangerously explosive temper.
- ✧ Is physically violent.
- ✧ Talks to you in a degrading or abusive manner.

Above all, dating—and falling in love—should make you feel good about yourself and elevate your mood. Although no relationship is completely free from moments of frustration and disappointment, if you often feel bad when you're around the person you think you love, you need to move on. And if the relationship is ever physically violent, talk to a parent, counselor, or other trusted adult about it.

What Does It Mean?

What does it mean when you—as a teenager—are in love with someone? Since you know (and you must realize this even if you don't want to accept it fully) that this person probably isn't the one you'll spend the rest of your life with, being in love at this age marks a certain progression:

- ✧ You've developed an important, ongoing relationship; dating isn't an isolated event anymore.

✧ You've moved forward from a casual friendship to a relationship that includes attraction and, probably, the
desire for physical affection.

A memorable song from Andrew Lloyd Weber's musical
Aspects of Love says it all in its title: "Love—Love Changes
Everything!" Being in love changes you and your outlook on
life. It causes you to be acknowledged as a couple, it trans-
forms you from selfishness to selflessness, and it bestows
upon you the mantle of maturity. This is not to say that you
rush and fall in love with anyone you are dating. It's a natural evolution as a dating relationship changes into the ultimate seriousness. It gives you a chance to see what anyone
who has been in love experiences.

Once having been in love, you will never forget the feelings.
And, you will be able to recognize it when it comes again. Of
course every relationship is different in intensity and detail,
but common elements persist in a relationship in which two
people are in love.

However, love is both strong and fragile at the same time.
Above all, it must be cared for. It can be the most powerful of
human emotions while also being the most tenuous.

The Strength of Love

When you're in love, you no longer have to vie for your loved
one's affection or work so hard to make every moment fun.
Feelings of love can transcend time and space: You can be
away and still be in love, although it may not be the best way
to keep a love going. It is almost as if you passed over into a
safe sphere in which it is a "given" that you're within an important and relatively enduring relationship. Jason was 16 and
in love. And he loved being in love. He said, "Being in love
with Laura made this the most involved relationship I've had.
But, it was also the most relaxed. We just know how much
each of us cares for the other. I never have to worry about
whether Laura will go out with me; we're in love, and we're
always there for each other. It's like we swam through choppy
water and now got to the relaxed piece of the sandbar."

The Fragility of Love

Just because love can be a strong bond doesn't mean that you can leave the relationship untended. Above all else, you can never take it for granted—no one wants to be regarded as a fixture. Just as one can fall in love, one can fall out of love.

Time Out

Take the time to savor how special your love relationship can be. Continue to celebrate the romantic love that you both are privileged to have.

While being in love may give you some security, you cannot become less action-oriented. You will think about the other person a great deal; take some moments to think about why you have continued to be in love, and acknowledge to them that your feelings are still strong.

What Does Love Tell You About Yourself?

The amazing power of love is that—if you pay attention—you can gain profound insight into yourself. Being in love, especially for the first time, provides new emotions, experiences, and dreams for the future that will shape your personality and your inner being.

Making the transition from thinking about yourself to really thinking about another person helps you to mature and come into your own. Knowing how you can please and satisfy another human being gives you pleasure and satisfaction.

The Least You Need to Know

✧ Love has several varieties, but common elements.

✧ Love is a maturing experience, in which you pass from concerns about yourself to concerns about others.

✧ Love does change everything.

✧ Love has strength and fragility.

✧ Love requires care and nurturing.

Chapter 17

Staying in Love

In This Chapter

- ❖ Love involves work
- ❖ Love affects you
- ❖ Love affects your partner
- ❖ Love is learning

So you are in love. You probably feel just great, maybe a little nervous at times, about yourself and about the person you're with. You're also discovering that you've created a whole new entity—a relationship—that has a life of its own, that seems to grow and change a little bit every day.

But falling in love and staying in love are two very different matters. In order for the relationship to continue to grow, you've got to work at it a little bit. In this chapter, I'll explore the techniques for keeping this love relationship going. You'll see that it helps to reassess the relationship fairly often, so that you can reinforce what's working and spot problems before they undermine the positive aspects.

Discovering How to Stay in Love

Falling in love may seem as if it follows some kind of natural, predetermined course. When you find the right person, it doesn't take any planning or any work to fall in love—you meet, date, and then your feelings for each other begin to grow and flourish. Each of these stages has its own parameters and thresholds, and it is clear that you have to be ready for them. You will wind up dating many people, but you usually will fall in love with only a few. Timing and readiness are significant factors.

Record Book

Is falling in love a random, lucky event or is there some calculation required? When asked whether his discoveries were merely his being in the right place at the right time, the great French biologist Louis Pasteur supposedly remarked, "Chance favors the prepared mind!" So you may indeed fall in love by chance, but it helps to be prepared.

I've already discussed how it's almost impossible to define what it is about a particular person that makes you fall in love with him or her. Sometimes, a person simply affects you like no one else; he or she may simply delight you, and your relationship grows seamlessly the longer you're together. With some people, you may think you are in love on the first date! And in other relationships, it may take a long time to realize that what you really have together is a love affair.

Indeed, there have been many instances of two people who have become close friends—maybe over many years—and suddenly realize that they are actually in love. In fact, the deepest and most enduring relationships are always based in friendship. Sometimes love comes first; other times, it's the friendship that sets the pace of the relationship.

Chances are, you'll fall in love sometime with someone who doesn't return the feelings. But there's nothing like the moment when you realize that the one you love loves you back, and that you're both beginning to recognize how special you've become to each other. In most cases, that realization happens over time, after you've gotten to know each other pretty well and have spent some significant time together, enjoying day-to-day life in addition to the dating experience.

Just as falling in love requires some groundwork, staying in love necessitates even more action. By action, this means that you have to expend some energy in taking care of this relationship and keeping you both in love.

Penalty Flag

Don't neglect to set the stage for love. That means making sure that you're ready for the commitment a relationship requires. Falling in love is not simply letting loose and "falling"; it only really happens when you've set the stage for it.

If you want to keep the relationship going, you're going to have to concentrate on several different aspects. You must make sure you both continue to care for each other—and show that care and love in big and small ways. You have to keep striving to learn more about each other—what you think, what you want now and in the future, and how you feel.

Keep Building Your Relationship

As discussed, it's important to recognize that you and your loved one have created something new: a relationship. And it is this entity that you need to care for and continue to build. This relationship life needs to be nurtured, watered, fertilized, and tended to in order for it to succeed. Just because it's a relationship bonded by love does not mean that it can get by with less attention. In fact, the more love involved, the more care that's required.

Instant Replay

Sherry was 18 and ecstatic to be in love with Marco, also 18. But now she looks back at that relationship with some sadness. "I simply took Marco for granted. I knew that we had reached the stage where we loved each other. I certainly was sure of my love for him, and I thought I was sure of his love for me. But, we simply grew too used to each other. I made little treats for him much less frequently, and he no longer brought me flowers every week. It was almost like—well, we were in love, so we didn't need to impress each other any more. I thought it would last forever. I didn't realize that Marco could ever just fall out of love as well."

Continuing to build a relationship means moving along to deepen what you have together. It means continuing to build passion, commitment, and intimacy. It means continuing to do all the things you did as you began to create a relationship together—and that includes the joys of dating, having fun, learning about each other, and learning about yourself.

Once you decide to move forward in this way, you have to work at it and foster it.

In fact, it may sound a bit silly, but you need to continue to have dates with someone with whom you are in love. If you just assume you and your date are together and don't plan special events and activities, you'll soon grow bored with one another. See each occasion together as a singular event in which you can have time together to enjoy and increase your knowledge of each other.

Care for Each Other

It may seem redundant to say that if you're in love you have to care for the person you love. But, so many people forget to show affection and to pay close attention to the needs of that special person in their lives, and that's what it takes: constant attention. When things are going well, you must celebrate the good times with your partner. When there is adversity, help each other withstand the pain.

In fact, it may be that getting through the tough times will end up being more meaningful to you and your relationship than anything else. Having to go through some bad times is difficult; but having someone with you to share the burden is invaluable. This is often the measure of the love of one person for another. And the inability of one partner to be really there for another can impair the bond between them.

Caring for each other also needs to be expressed in small ways as well as big ones. Small gestures of regard or affection are huge in the recipient's eyes. Bringing someone a little gift, writing them a note, or giving them a single flower are simple but amazingly effective ways of signaling your regard and love. Victorian women would never let their beloved husbands go to their offices without giving them fresh-cut garden blossoms for the buttonholes in their lapels; this was a tiny but significant gesture of love.

Instant Replay

Debbie and Max were both 16 and they were crazy about each other. Debbie loved Max for many reasons, but the smallest thing, for her, was the biggest. Debbie loved poetry, and Max showered Debbie with verse. At first he copied poems out of an anthology, but after a bit, he tried to write some himself. He wasn't very good, but he was very motivated. She remembered his poems, imperfect as they were, as the purest way in which he tried to delight her.

Lust for Knowledge

All relationships involve learning about your partner, and love relationships are no less the case. To keep the love alive, you need to lust for knowledge about your partner: what they like, where they came from, where they are going, and how they think. Discovering that you're in love doesn't mean that you know all there is to know about the object of your affection; on the contrary, it signifies that you can now begin to delve even further into the world of your partner.

When you're in love, there should be very few areas that are out-of-bounds. The more you know about someone, the more involved with him or her you can be. You want to know how to make him or her happy, which requires the same open lines of communication that you needed to get the relationship going in the first place.

Take Lois and Buzz. The nicest times in their relationship were the hours they spent together quietly talking. They discussed their dreams, hopes, dilemmas, and joys; they even laughed about their own faults. The talk reflected the inner-most thoughts and feelings of each person. This served to confirm and in some ways correct the image each partner had of the other. And, as they shared these intimate dreams, they grew closer: The words expanded the picture of the other person, and the very act of communication fostered bonding.

Self-Exposition

Self-exposition is another word for revelation: When it comes to fostering a healthy relationship, nothing counts more than letting your loved one get to know the real you. You need to be willing to be yourself—even to be vulnerable.

Allow the real you to come forth. When you are in love, you will want to have this person as someone who can be there for you in times of concern. And those times may sometimes arise because of your own mistakes. Perhaps the best part of being in love is the fact that you no longer have to rely on pretense or role-playing. Your partner loves you for who you really are—mistakes, faults, and all.

Keeping Tabs

Continuing to stay in love means continuing to look at your relationship to reconfirm your feelings about it and the role you play in it. Periodically, you need to step back, savor the relationship for what it brings you both, and honestly exam-ine what the love aspect of your relationship is. Take Hank, for instance. He was an extremely organized person. At 16, he was junior class president, and could be relied on to take charge of any problem. He was in love with Julie, also 16. He loved to talk to her every Sunday night about their relation-ship. However, this was not an endless discourse on where their relationship was going. Hank used his Sunday nights to think about how much he really continued to love Julie and why. And he used his conversation time with her to tell her that. For Julie, it was a weekly dose of verbal heaven.

The most important rule when it comes to reassessing the state of your relationship is to be honest at all times. Furthermore, you have to act on what you've discovered. Reassessment is useless if it is not linked to practical action. If there are some warning signs, they need to be confronted and dealt with. If the relationship is moving southward, you have to ask why and begin to explore whether it's appropriate to move on, or if it's worth salvaging.

Love Changes You

Being in love with someone brings to you a wealth of new emotions and feelings. In thinking about the value and intensity of a love relationship, you need to open yourself up to experience it. You stay in love because of the pleasure that love brings to you; but you need to be able to recognize that pleasure.

Approach looking at what love does for you by looking at the positives. Ask yourself, "How have I changed by being in love with my partner?" Of course, you may have some negativity about being less inclined to spend free time with your old friends, but the advantages of being in love should clearly win out. If they don't, the reassessment has uncovered some problems which you had best work on.

Usually, you take a look at how love changes you with the hope that that relationship will continue. But even if it doesn't, staying in love for a time brings you awareness of the ultimate of human emotions. It will allow you to approach future relationships with the confidence that knowledge (what being in love is like) brings.

Being in love affects your partner as well. If it's the right kind of relationship, he or she will feel happier and more secure because of you. Passion—for you, for life, and for new experiences and interests—may also be a fine side effect of being in love. Meg, 16, was in love with Lou, 17. What seemed most extraordinary to her was how being in love affected Lou. "Before we fell in love, Lou seemed to be a self-absorbed jock who only seemed to care about how he looked, how he played, and how he did on tests. He was obsessed about getting into the best college. But then, he fell in love with me. I saw him transform into a person who was caring about someone else, and was really concerned about whether I was happy. I don't know what will happen when he goes off to college; our relationship will probably end. But, he has made me happy, and I feel I have given him a gift, making him a more complete person."

Sustaining a love relationship teaches you some very important lessons, including …

- ✧ You're growing up and coming into yourself.
- ✧ You can foster a positive relationship.
- ✧ You can learn about yourself and someone you care about.

There is something mature about being in love. And there is something equally mature about being able to stay in love. One of the tasks of adulthood is to gravitate toward a singular love. Being in love and keeping it going gives you an experience in the adult world, and serves as a foundation for future love experiences. Even if you think of yourself as falling in and out of love rather quickly, you have begun to think about love, and the impact it has on you, on someone special, and on the couple you become within a relationship. And this serves to prepare you for future relationships by being able to assess whether the next one is "the real thing."

Falling in love confirms that you can take a relationship to a serious level. Staying in love implies that you can actually master the relationship. Relationships are almost alive: You can nourish a relationship, see it grow, and sustain it. And you do this through your own action and energy. You will never approach any relationship—or even casual dating situation—with the same perspective you had before you were in love.

Staying in love gives you insight into who you are and what you can bring to an interaction with another person. You have learned about yourself and experience what amazing capabilities you have. The abilities you have to love and be loved—and to keep it going—let you see yourself as a capable, maturing, and caring young adult.

The Least You Need to Know

✧ Staying in love requires you to take an active role.

✧ Sustaining love involves falling back on the techniques used to build good relationships.

✧ Reassessing your love is important.

✧ Being able to sustain a love relationship will help you learn how to become a healthy, satisfied adult.

Sexuality and Sex

In This Chapter

✧ Sexuality as a part of who you are

✧ What sex is and isn't

✧ Sex as a part of the dating game

✧ How sex affects you and your partner

If you're like most teens, you began playing the dating game hoping you'd end up in a relationship—a relationship with someone you cared about deeply, who returned your affection. You have learned a good deal about others in this process, and have discovered many new things about yourself. With a little luck and a lot of hard work, you've fallen in love with someone, and have made the relationship work for you both.

Perhaps from the very start of the relationship, and certainly by now, you've been thinking about this person not only in a romantic way, but also in a sexual way. That's perfectly normal. In fact, sexuality—how each person expresses his or her qualities as a male or female—is an integral part of one's personality. What you are attracted to is not only someone's looks, intelligence, and charm, but also his or her sexuality.

Now, that's not to say that every couple in a romantic relationship expresses themselves sexually—far from it. Many teens choose not to have sex until they are much older and in a committed relationship. However, that doesn't mean that sex isn't on their minds, or that physical intimacy of some type—kissing, holding hands, or cuddling—doesn't take place. In this chapter, I'll take a look at sex and how it shapes a relationship and the two people in it.

What Is Sex?

Sex may mean different things to different people. Although the mention of the word "sex" may have brought on an embarrassed laugh when you were eleven, it takes on a bit of seriousness when you begin dating. But it is important to be clear what we mean by sex.

For many people, sex is equivalent to sexual intercourse, and studies that cite the number of teens who have had sex mean the number of those who have had intercourse. But the word "sex" actually has three quite separate definitions:

✧ Gender

✧ Physical characteristics

✧ The act of physical intimacy, including intercourse

I'll discuss them one by one.

Gender

Sex is the equivalent of gender, as in the question "What sex are you?" which you have to check on the SAT application form. It refers formally to whether you are a male or female in terms of your anatomical features. But the gender concept also includes how you come across to others and yourself as a male or female. It implies how you feel as a male or female. It may even include some understanding of the differences between the sexes.

Physical Characteristics

Sex implies a consideration of the physical self and the human body, and how it appears to another person. Of course, this image may not at all times reflect the more standard ideas of the general public. Sex also refers to the reproductive system—the primary and secondary sexual characteristics in men and women, such as breasts, genitalia, and pubic hair.

Instant Replay

Annette was 16 and quite beautiful by most standards. She had a magnificent face, an outstanding figure, gorgeous features, and was a nice person in addition. But one admirer really thought of her as "sexy" for a different reason. Not because she exuded appeal and attractiveness, nor because of her physical or personal beauty, but because of her ability to communicate well with anyone and make everyone feel at ease. Annette's personality traits made her an incredibly attractive female to whom others gravitated. This was as powerful an element of attraction as her face or figure.

Physical Intimacy

Sex is also a term used to connote acts of physical, sexual intimacy. Just as it is incorrect to equate sex exclusively with the act of sexual intercourse, sex must be considered a spectrum of activity. Is kissing a sexual act? How about touching someone? Can one hold hands with another and claim that they are engaging in sex?

Evan, age 16, felt as if he had a sexual relationship with the girl he was dating. They did a lot of "making out" with much passionate kissing; they even touched each other. He talked with his friends a lot and was very proud of his sexual relationship with his girlfriend. "After all," he explained, "we kiss each other a lot and hold each other. It makes me feel real close to her. To me that's sex. So it isn't going 'all the way' yet, but some of the way is still sex to me!"

If sex is a physical expression of oneself and one's maleness or femaleness, then the term "sex" may define a wide variety of activities, from holding hands to actual intercourse.

Sex is a form of individual expression, as well as a way of expressing love and affection. Just as there are no two snowflakes that are identical, there are no two people who express themselves—and their sexuality—in exactly the same way. Your sexual style may change in time as you grow older and become more experienced.

Record Book

A simple touch evokes powerful human emotions. Studies of tiny premature babies in the newborn intensive care nursery show that those babies who are touched and stroked, even if they are too small or too sick to be actually held, do much better than babies who are not touched. There is something about touch that allows humans—and some animals such as cats and dogs—to perceive attachment and closeness.

Is Sex a Natural Part of Dating?

Sex as described as physical intimacy with another person should be pleasurable. It is an act of giving and receiving pleasure through touch. Although you do not necessarily need physical interaction to give and receive pleasure from another person, if you're both ready and comfortable, touching can add to the pleasure of being with one another. In the next chapter, we'll discuss how to decide whether or not to be sexually involved.

Instant Replay

Renee, age 15, just loves it when Randy holds her hand. "I can't tell you what I feel. But when I feel Randy's hand feeling mine, I feel Randy being so close to me." Many others agree with Renee's excitement. Long before you and she were born, the classic rock group The Beatles recorded a song about the power of touching called "I Want to Hold Your Hand."

It's important to note, however, that physical intimacy of any kind is an important step that you shouldn't take without considering its ramifications with care. Remember, just being together without any physical contact can have its own magic. There are couples in love who enjoy just being in the same room with each other. To them, knowing that the other person is near them is delightful in itself. They do not require touching to confirm their regard for one another.

Dating can include several aspects of sexual expression. There is usually some aspect of sexual attraction always present in a dating relationship. You find someone alluring because you also find his or her physical being alluring. You may also find his or her mind or the fact that he or she is kindhearted is "sexy." And you are usually stimulated when you think of those attributes.

Is Everyone Doing It?

If by "it" you mean sexual intercourse, the answer is actually "no." Less than 50 percent of 16-year-olds have had intercourse; by age 19 there are still 25 percent who have not. While sexual intercourse is a measure of sexual experience, one episode of sexual intercourse is only one experience. Having had intercourse does not mean that you continue to be sexually active or are very experienced. Having intercourse may be a singular event with a singular partner.

For many young people, their first intercourse experience is not always optimal. They may have chosen to have intercourse with a partner with whom they didn't have a genuinely affectionate relationship, or because they felt that intercourse was the next logical step in the relationship, but didn't feel comfortable or ready. At times young people are actually turned off by the sexual experience, and decide to wait until they are in love for the next encounter.

More teens experience holding, kissing, petting, or other varied activities short of intercourse. Kissing and holding are often part of a dating relationship. You don't need to have intercourse: Kissing in itself can be quite magical. Rick, now close to 50 years old, still remembers what it was like to kiss the first girl he fell in love with. He remembers where they were and what she wore the first time he kissed her. It was an awkward first good-night kiss, but for him it awoke him to the more physical pleasures of dating someone he cared about.

Oral sex has become a more common activity of some young people. But this is an intensely intimate activity which can be as emotionally involving as intercourse and fraught with some of the same physical concerns in the potential spread of sexually transmitted diseases.

What Happens to Your Relationship After Sex?

Expressing your sexuality with another person brings a relationship to a new height. Whether your relationship includes kissing and hugging, or whether it has progressed to sexual intercourse, physical intimacy will change your relationship.

Penalty Flag

Don't assume that everyone thinks about sex the way you do. People have their own individual notions of what sex means to them, to others, and to their partnerships. And your view of sex may also change, depending on where your relationship happens to be; it may also change with different relationships.

Sex can have two effects on a relationship: It can either intensify or diminish it. In the next two sections, I'll take a look at each.

It Intensifies

In most cases of committed relationships in which both parties carefully consider the ramifications beforehand, sex moves a relationship to a higher level. The physical connection that sex brings deepens the emotional and interpersonal intimacy of a relationship. Marina was 17. Her relationship with Misha had progressed from a merely dating relationship to one in which they had begun touching a lot. They kissed each other, explored each other's bodies, and moved on to having sexual intercourse. Marina said, "By having Misha so intimately involved with me and me with him, I feel we have become much more committed. It's no longer a date and then 'see ya.' It's a real relationship, just like adults have. Sex has sort of cemented us together."

While the physical relationship may expand and deepen your relationship, it does not come without risks—both emotional and physical. The physical risks are quite serious: Not only do you have to protect yourself against pregnancy, you also have to be aware of the risks of sexually transmitted diseases.

The emotional risks stem from the fact that sexual intercourse is an incredibly intimate act that—if both partners are ready and feel the same way about creating a committed relationship—can deepen and expand the way two people communicate. On the other hand, if one person thinks of sex as a purely physical act while his or her partner is on another wavelength, the emotional fallout can be devastating.

It Diminishes

There are some cases in which sex actually causes the relationship to weaken and even to fall apart. If you're not sure that it's a step you want to take, sex can make you feel guilty and uncertain. It can even lower your self-esteem if you choose a partner who is not kind to you, or doesn't feel the same way about sex as you do.

If one party regards a sexual experience as just another opportunity to "score," and the other party doesn't share this philosophy, someone is going to feel very let down. Hopefully, both parties perceive sex to be an opportunity to give and receive pleasure within the context of love and affection, if not commitment.

Is Your Relationship a Partnership?

A sexual relationship is a relationship between two people. And these two people are partners. Their experience in dating has moved their relationship onward to include physical expression. As marvelous as this is, it is important to go back to the reasons you engage in relationships in the first place—to get to know your partner and yourself a little better.

Instant Replay

Gabe was 16 and regarded his relationship with his girl-friend Kate, also 16, as having entered into another phase. "Before we started getting into a lot of making out, things were a little simpler. I really like her a lot, and I think I actually love her, but I don't know. I am getting more involved with her physically, and that seems to be taking over the main part of our interaction these days. She likes it, and so do I. We are actually thinking of going all the way. But we used to talk easily a lot more. It seems as if I am really into touching her body so much—almost like that's the main reason right now to be together."

Sex brings this quest for knowledge to a much more complicated level. The first kiss may elevate a relationship in one party's eyes to something very different. It may imply a deepened level of partnership. And it may give you insights into how you come across to your partner as a sexually expressive person.

At the same time, it is crucial that you keep your eyes on your partner, who may be experiencing something quite different than you are. His or her feelings must be paramount to you—that's what love and commitment really mean.

It is important to learn from your sexual interactions, and the best way to do that is to keep open those lines of communication between you and your partner. Find out what pleases your partner and follow his or her lead as you explore the boundaries of your relationship. And, when it comes to the acts of intimacy themselves, giving feedback to your partner is a gift: It will help him or her provide pleasure to you. Intimacy is very much a partnership event.

Time Out

Aim to please. When it comes to physical intimacy, your goal should be to make your partner feel safe, secure, and adored. That means taking cues from him or her about how far to take the intimacy and when to back off.

The Least You Need to Know

◆ Sex means different things to different people at different times in each relationship.

◆ Physical intimacy involves a wide spectrum of actions.

◆ Sex is an expression of one's individuality.

◆ Sex between loving and committed partners usually deepens a relationship.

Chapter 19

Ready
or Not?

In This Chapter

✧ Relating sex to love

✧ Knowing when you are ready

✧ Decision-making

✧ Making the first time great

✧ Acting maturely

Sexuality is part of every human experience—it's not something you can avoid. But you can choose when you express yourself sexually to another person, and that choice is always yours and yours alone to make.

By this time, you may find yourself in a committed relationship with someone you really care for and are attracted to. You find yourself interested in exploring your sexuality within this trusted relationship. Perhaps you're considering oral sex or sexual intercourse. How do you know when you are ready for these next steps? In this chapter, I'll help you explore the issue of readiness when it comes to sexual experience.

Know the Difference Between Love and Sex

The differences between sex and love aren't always easy to define, but it's important to realize that they are quite significant. Sex can be fun, exciting, and passionate, but—believe it or not—if performed at the wrong time or with the wrong person, it can be boring or even depressing. And when it comes to love, well, that's a state of being that's impossible to define, at least in part because everyone in love defines it a bit differently, according to his or her individual background and experience.

The problem is, if you can't define the differences between physical intimacy and love, how do you know if you are in love with someone or just attracted sexually?

Love actually has many dimensions that encompass many feelings. Elements of love include:

- ✧ You feel attracted to, but also like, the person.
- ✧ You have a close friendship with him or her.
- ✧ You are deeply concerned about the care and well-being of that person.
- ✧ You treat that person well.
- ✧ You have intense feelings for him or her—sexual and emotional—and a desire for physical closeness.
- ✧ You may also be nervous or anxious.

Feelings themselves can't be the only deciding factor in a loving relationship. You have to think about other issues as well, such as whether the person is suitable for you in terms of his or her background, interests, and availability. Some kids can choose someone who is irresponsible or emotionally very immature or unethical; this may not be the best choice if you want to share a loving and sexual relationship.

Many people feel that love and sex have to be combined—that you need mutual respect and warmth in order to enjoy sex. Love increases the pleasure of sex and emphasizes the commonality of friendship. Psychologist Erich Fromm cites four components of love: care, responsibility, respect, and knowledge. These are also the components of a satisfactory sexual relationship.

Record Book

Founding father of psychiatry Sigmund Freud said in 1953 that love and sex were very much the same, linking the psychological with the physical. It was his contention that they could not be separated. Colleague Theodor Reik, however, contended that love and sex were separate, with sex being a biological function, and love a quest for emotional satisfaction.

Under the right circumstances, sex can be quite enjoyable! Most people enjoy touching and giving and receiving physical pleasure. Exploring your own feelings, physical and emotional, while getting to know someone else intimately can also be lots of fun. Indeed, sex has many fun aspects to it, but it also can be very emotionally charged and laden with physical and emotional consequences.

Time to See if It's Time

There comes a time for all young people to consider whether they should move forward in a relationship to include more advanced sexual experiences. All kids want to feel normal and want to fit in with their peer groups. There is pressure to join the peer culture, or even use sex as a weapon to rebel against what you know your parents don't want. You need to ask yourself if your decision fits your values, and assess the consequences. You need to be true to yourself and resist being manipulated by others. You do not have to compromise on this one. And you do not need others to approve of your own moral framework!

Penalty Flag

Don't make judgments about the decisions other kids make about sex. Some young people wish to postpone intercourse until marriage for religious, moral, and/or personal reasons. Others feel ready to explore sexuality. No matter what decision you've made for yourself, you have no right to judge the quality of another's decision in this highly personal area.

Take Kara, for example. Kara was 15 and wanted to be popular. Unfortunately, she thought the only way to get a boyfriend was to engage in increasingly sexual relationships. "It is what the boys expect nowadays in order to be their girlfriends. I don't really like it, but I feel that it is the only way a boy will continue to ask me out."

If you've ever felt like Kara, or if you're just unsure of where you stand in the teen world of sexuality, read on.

How to Know if You Are Ready

The first rule of sexual exploration is to never do something that doesn't feel right to you. The limits you put on your sexuality are your decision, based on your own principles. Even if you are in love with someone and you want to please him or her, you need to be true to yourself first. No one who is really!" in love with you would pressure you to do something that is against your personal beliefs.

Instant Replay

Antonio was 16 and was trying to convince his girlfriend to have intercourse with him. "I told her there was nothing to it but a fun experience for both of us. I could make her feel like a woman, and we could both have some enjoyment. It's not like it means that much. Lots of people go to bed just because it's fun to do. It doesn't have to be so heavy." But Marie, also 16, felt otherwise: "I know that sex will be fun. But to me it has some other meaning as well. He just doesn't seem to understand that using sex just to have fun is just not right for me. If he wants to have fun, let's just go dancing!"

Kristin, for instance, was feeling pressured by Todd to have sexual intercourse. She had told him many times that she wouldn't feel comfortable having sex until she was in college; this decision was a big step for her and she wanted to be sure it was right. Todd had professed his love for her on many occasions, but lately was becoming more persistent in asking for intercourse. Kristin had a sudden realization: "He says he loves me, but he cannot accept something I believe in which is so basic to me. He really wants me to forget who I am. How can someone who says they love me want me to do that?"

Readiness to have oral sex or intercourse requires you to look at your own principles. Is this even a question you can discuss with your partner, or do your own rules warrant you tabling this issue for now? If you really feel committed to sexual intercourse only after marriage, it is provocative and impractical to debate the intercourse issue now. Just simply tell your partner your limits and expect him or her to respect those limits. If you lose a partner because of it, better that than lose your self-respect and deny your principles.

This is a very personal decision. When making it, weigh the pros and the cons by asking yourself these ten pertinent questions for assessing readiness:

- ✧ Can you talk to your partner about this?
- ✧ Do you feel secure with your partner?
- ✧ Do you trust that your partner does not have multiple partners and is not a carrier of sexually transmitted diseases?
- ✧ Are you prepared with birth control and have you thought about what would happen if a pregnancy resulted?
- ✧ Are you sexually attracted to your partner?
- ✧ Do you feel physically ready?
- ✧ Are you both knowledgeable about sexual technique?
- ✧ Do you love your partner?
- ✧ Does your partner love you?
- ✧ Will you feel all right the next day because this is consistent with your personal values?

You need to have enough positive answers to the ten questions to confirm that you are ready to have your first sexual intercourse experience. Again, sex involves both psychological and physical elements. It is amazing and indescribable, both normal and natural. It has to be your decision, and you have to be in control before you begin. You should look at the questions and decide which of them are really deal-breakers for you. For instance, you may not be too knowledgeable about technique, but you do not ever want to compromise your values.

As you learn more about yourself, you will better understand your own sexual feelings and concerns. You will also understand how these feelings fit into your whole life, spiritually, intellectually, and psychologically. Think about how to develop ideas for dealing with your sexual drives. You don't have to have intercourse; there are other ways to express feelings in dating relationships.

Talk to your friends, your parents, and other family members. Be true to your own feelings toward your partner and to your own value systems.

How to Say "No"

Saying "no" is not always easy. There is the inevitable pressure to go along with what a sizable number of your peers who are sexually active are doing. Remember that not everyone is having intercourse; but it may seem (though it isn't always true) that the "cool" kids are the ones who are doing so.

When you say "no," you might want to do it in a reasonable, objective way. Sam was 16 and decided that he really was not ready to have intercourse yet. He had some religious convictions that were not encouraging of this behavior. He was really not sure he was in love with his girlfriend, at least he did not feel what he always had dreamed being in love would make him feel. And he was concerned about how much he really knew about sex and whether he could make this first time for him and his partner very special.

Sam had four options in announcing his decision in this matter. First, Sam could announce to the world that he had religious principles that precluded him from having intercourse yet, but he was concerned that it would make him appear as if he was overly moralistic and self-righteous. And his religion did not prohibit it, but simply discouraged it.

Second, Sam could excuse his reluctance by admitting that he did not feel a special love for his girlfriend, but he did not want to open up that dialogue at this time. Besides, Sam was really not sure if he *was* actually falling in love with her but just a little more slowly.

Penalty Flag

Don't obsess about the decision. There is actually something liberating about making a decision and moving on. One of the most vexing circumstances for all of us is indecision. Deliberation may take on its own life and become totally consuming. Just move on until it's time to reconsider.

Third, Sam could confirm that he felt awkward about the process of intercourse, but he saw no reason to embarrass himself with his friends.

What Sam did elect to do is a fourth option. Sam told his girlfriend and his friends: "Look, I'm just not ready to go all the way yet. I regard it as an important thing and it is for me an important decision." The statement was direct and definitive. He saw no reason to justify anything to anyone. He saw only the need to state where he was on the issue, and he framed it in terms of this being a personal decision for him.

Saying "no" does not mean always having to explain yourself. You do not have to justify your decision to anyone but yourself. Sexuality will be with you all your life; you do not have to have sex now.

Enjoy Your Decision

Remember that decisions occur at one particular time. Circumstances may change, your relationship may change, and you may make a different decision as time goes on. But for now you have elected what you want to do. In this situation, a decision not to have intercourse merely postpones a decision to have first intercourse to some later time. But you may be at a different place later, perhaps with a different person.

Time Out

Always remember you can say "no" anytime. Just because you've had sex once (or more than once) with one partner doesn't mean you have to continue to do so if you now feel uncomfortable. And, should you move on to another partner, the decision to have sex for the first time with him or her should be considered just as important as the very, very first time you made the decision.

Remember the First Time

The first time is usually memorable. It may not necessarily be all that you wanted, it may be more wonderful than you dreamed, or it may be blurred by indistinct images. Despite the outcome, it is usually an event you remember, just as you remember your first kiss or first love.

When it comes to the first time, the most important rule to follow is to communicate openly and honestly with your partner. You also need to listen as he or she tells you about him- or herself and his or her own issues. This is no time for bravado or trying to demonstrate your wealth of experience. This is a special time in one or both of your lives—a time to create a lasting impression.

Behave Responsibly and Maturely

Always remember the importance of being a mature person who is sensitive to the needs of your partner. For many people, sexual intercourse is a major step in their lives. This is something they have thought about or fantasized about for a long time.

Intercourse often changes people's perceptions of themselves. Some young people feel that they have finally achieved an adult milestone, and can now understand what the real adult world of sexual relationships is all about. Some people feel let down, confused that there is not more to it that they thought. Some sense that this is a reason to celebrate that they have really become a man or a woman. Others may feel awkward, or even feel a sense of shame. There are lots of feelings conjured up when you are sexually active, and, as a participant and a partner, you must be sensitive to them.

Instant Replay

Bob had his first sexual experience at 18 with Carol, a fellow senior in high school whom he liked, but did not really love. But Carol assumed that intercourse meant love. Bob saw this as the culmination of his relationship with Carol before he went off to college and to new adventures. Carol was under the impression that this activity ushered a new level of seriousness into their relationship. Assumptions were made because communication was absent. Bob had wanted to "get laid" before he graduated, and Carol was a willing partner. He did not, however, discuss his plan with Carol. Afterward, when Carol brought up the topic of remaining exclusive, even though they were going to colleges far away from each other, she was rebuffed by Bob, who saw their "encounter" only as the beginning of his experiences in real manhood. In the end, Carol felt hurt, humiliated, and guilty.

Sex by itself does not signify maturity. You have to act with a strong sense of self and regard for others in order to be considered mature. Mature people in a mature relationship care about each other's feelings and behave responsibly. When sex comes into the picture, a couple needs to communicate more openly than ever. You need to be honest and make your feelings clear. You need to listen and to hear what your partner tells you. You don't tell someone that you love him or her if you don't. If intercourse means little to you in the way of emotional ties, tell that to your partner in advance so that they can be given an opportunity to assess whether this attitude is something they can live with. Before you have sex, make sure the two of you can act with maturity, caring, and compassion.

The Least You Need to Know

✧ Sex is far more meaningful when it is associated with a loving relationship.

✧ Knowing when you are ready is an individual assessment based on your own values and dreams.

✧ Sexual intercourse for most people is important, and may be charged with many psychological issues.

✧ You can say "no" at any time in any relationship.

✧ The first time may be a significant occasion for one or both parties. It takes careful planning and preparation.

✧ Being honest with yourself and your partner is crucial.

Chapter 20

Know the Score: Be Careful!

In This Chapter

✧ Birth control as a practical issue

✧ The dangers of sexually transmitted diseases

✧ The specter of HIV/AIDS

✧ Accidental pregnancy

✧ Emotional fallout

You've decided to have a sexual relationship, including sexual intercourse. Doing so, you've made what you must make sure is an adult and mature decision. Your partner must also make the decision to progress to sexual intimacy with some care. Both of you will share in a great responsibility, and it's up to you to make sure this is an adult and mature decision, which requires you to think about things in an adult way. You both have to think of the emotional and physical consequences of having sexual intercourse, and that includes understanding how to prevent pregnancy and the transmission of sexual diseases.

In this chapter, I'll look at some of the issues facing sexually active people, including teens. Birth control is a basic concern for all heterosexual couples having intercourse. Sexually transmitted diseases remain epidemic, with the HIV infection striking many young people every day. I'll give you some tips so that you can protect yourself if you've decided to take this important step.

For Every Action There Is a Reaction

When you're a little kid, say three or four years old, you're just beginning to understand that when you perform a certain action, touching a hot stove, for instance, a reaction occurs, and one that isn't necessarily pleasant—ouch! As you get older, your thinking becomes even more sophisticated when you realize that if you have a host of choices, each of those choices may have very different consequences.

To have or to abstain from sexual intercourse is one of those choices. Either way, there will be consequences. The more serious and immediate consequences come from choosing to have sex. As we discussed in Chapter 19, "Ready or Not?" making that decision requires that you then plan with care how to protect yourself from the physical and emotional fallout that could occur. It may seem romantic and exciting to "go with the flow" and let things move along spontaneously; however, nothing is less romantic than an unplanned pregnancy or a deadly disease.

If it is your decision to pursue sexual intercourse, you want to be able to do so with a sense of enjoyment. It actually diminishes the pleasure by worrying about the consequences of these activities. It is especially significant because there are ways to minimize the risks in this potentially risky behavior.

Preventing Pregnancy

I begin here with a simple rule: If you don't use birth control all the time, it is just a matter of time before you become pregnant. If this is not what you want, you need to use birth control each and every time you have sexual intercourse. Healthy young people are biologically adapted to reproduce. Not using birth control means that you are gambling on nature not doing what it is supposed to do. Why would you want to take such odds?

Instant Replay

Meg was in love with Roger. They decided, at 17, that they were ready to have sexual intercourse. But passion got the better of them and they neglected to use a condom. It was like playing roulette on that very first occasion for both of them—and they lost. Meg became pregnant. What started out as a romantic and important occasion for them ended up as a terrible dilemma. They now had many new decisions to make, with many new emotional consequences to face. Roger and Meg were 17, but really not ready to assume the adult responsibilities of sexual intercourse, which includes using protection in every encounter.

There are reasons why teens don't use birth control consistently:

◆ They do not believe that anything can happen.

◆ They really want to test the system.

◆ They think it decreases the pleasure or displeases their partner.

◆ They want to become pregnant.

Many teens have not yet accepted the fact that an action may have consequences for them. They know bad things happen, but they just don't think it will happen to them. Some teens think they're invincible, that they can beat the odds no matter how high the deck is stacked against them. Nothing is further from the truth. Each time you tempt fate by not using protection is a challenge to get caught.

Record Book

The great educator Jean Piaget described in 1924 how our thought processes develop through childhood into adulthood. Before the teen years, children engage in a process of concrete operations; they think only of what happens now. During adolescence, teens begin the process of formal operations, in which they can consider things like cause-and-effect and can understand that a given action may yield a given consequence some time in the future. However, all teenagers do not go through this at identical times.

There are several methods of birth control accessible to teenagers. Of course, the most basic and the absolute safest method is abstaining from sex altogether. The easiest and the best method is using condoms, each and every time. Condoms not only prevent pregnancy, but they also provide protection against most sexually transmitted diseases. Condoms may save your life, in that they offer reasonable protection from the HIV virus that causes AIDS. Condoms are available even in grocery stores these days, and both young men and young women can buy them and make sure the male partner uses them during intercourse.

Penalty Flag

Use a condom each and every time. No one should engage in sexual intercourse without at least using a condom. This is absolute. When used properly, a condom will protect against pregnancy and sexually transmitted diseases.

There are also other methods of birth control to consider. Contraceptive pills, implants, or long-acting injections are various combinations of hormones to prevent ovulation—the egg being released from the ovary—or to make the uterus unsuitable for implantation of a fertilized egg. Diaphragms or cervical caps are used with contraceptive jellies to act as a barrier to sperm entry into the uterus. None of these methods protect against sexually transmitted diseases, however, and so should be your choice only if you are in a long-term, committed relationship with someone you trust. All of these are things that can be discussed confidentially with your own physician or at clinics such as Planned Parenthood.

There are assorted other methods that are far less reliable. "Coitus interruptus," or withdrawal before ejaculation, is not recommended because some semen can seep out of the penis and into the uterus during intercourse. The so-called "rhythm method," which consists of trying to abstain from sex during the most fertile time in a woman's cycle (about the middle) is also unreliable, because the precise time of ovulation is difficult to determine. Having unprotected intercourse may lead you to seek help for pregnancy prevention by requesting from a healthcare provider the "morning-after pill," which contains hormones that prevent a fertilized egg from implanting in the uterus. You need to speak with the provider about the pros and cons of this pill, along with the potential side effects.

Time Out

Show your love by providing protection. If two people care about each other, they'll do whatever it takes to keep each other safe and healthy. How can someone who supposedly loves you have intercourse without regard to keeping you out of harm's way? Can this really then be love?

Preventing Sexually Transmitted Diseases

Microorganisms present in the genital area cause sexually transmitted diseases, or "STDs." They are spread through intimate contact with an infected partner during oral, anal, or genital sex. The most common types of sexually transmitted diseases include HIV/AIDS, gonorrhea, chlamydia, syphilis, genital herpes, genital warts, nongonococcal urethritis, crabs, scabies, and hepatitis B.

In addition to using condoms, you can also choose several other methods of protecting yourself from infection. First, abstinence can protect you from genital to genital contraction. Birth control pills can prevent you from becoming pregnant, but they will not prevent you from contracting an STD. Condoms offer the most effective method of prevention. It is also important to know your partner and know if they "sleep around." Finally, the more partners you have, the greater the chance of your encountering one who is capable of transferring an STD to you.

If you're having sex, it's up to you to pay close attention to your sexual health. That means staying alert to the symptoms of any and all sexually transmitted diseases. If you have any reason to believe that you've contracted an STD, see your doctor for treatment immediately. Left untreated, many STDs can lead to sterility in both men and women. It is important to have a high index of suspicion for having contracted a sexually transmitted disease.

Penalty Flag

Be aware that, when it comes to sexually transmitted diseases, you're not just having sex with your partner; you're also having sex with all the people he or she has ever been with. If one of those partners had an STD, your partner might be infected and able to pass that disease on to you.

Knowing the Truth About AIDS

Acquired Immune Deficiency Syndrome, or AIDS, is caused by infection with the HIV, or Human Immunodeficiency Virus. It is transmitted by sexual contact, or by use of contaminated needles in drug use. AIDS is an illness that weakens the immune system, which leaves your body susceptible to a variety of infections and cancers. The HIV organism, a virus, can infect someone without producing symptoms. However, anyone with HIV can infect another person through sexual or blood contact; the virus may be passed in secretions and in blood whenever unprotected sexual contact occurs.

There is as yet no cure for AIDS. Although there are drugs that have allowed people to delay the onset of deadly infections, the HIV is still present. There is also great concern that HIV infections will eventually become a major problem for teenagers who do not have responsible sex using condoms. HIV infection can occur with just one encounter. You cannot be relaxed about guarding against HIV.

Penalty Flag

Don't panic! Don't hide! Most STDs can be cured. Don't be embarrassed about having contracted an infection—this frequently happens to young people. But, above all, don't be a fool and not seek medical help! That is really dumb, for the earlier an infection is caught, the greater the likelihood that damage will be minimized.

Facing Pregnancy: What to Do When Birth Control Fails

Mistakes happen, and pregnancy can be the result of the mistake. The issues here boil down to decisions regarding what to do:

✧ Terminate

✧ Carry to term and keep the baby

✧ Carry to term and put the baby up for adoption

Termination

Pregnancy termination, or abortion, is a procedure that expels the product of conception from the uterus. While this procedure is a common and simple one, it is nonetheless a medical procedure that requires a skilled healthcare provider. Although abortion does terminate a pregnancy, it should not be regarded as a method of birth control.

Record Book

Nearly all patients who are HIV-positive recall having engaged in unprotected sex or in intravenous drug use. Because HIV is a peculiar virus, some people are quickly infected while others may be slightly more immune. The fact is that no one knows how he or she will be affected, so you must be protected at every sexual encounter.

Delivery and Keeping the Baby

Another choice is to carry the baby to delivery and to keep it. The baby may be raised by you, your partner, both of you, or a member of your family. A requirement for you is to care for yourself—and your unborn baby—during your pregnancy: Eat well, see a healthcare provider, and take vitamins.

Being a new parent will be very stressful at times. This is not consistent with most teenagers' activities. And you need to arrange for good childcare in order to continue your education and career development. Some young people are able to do fine—especially with help. Raising a child is a marvelous activity; but whether this is the right time for you to do this is a consideration that each person or couple must decide.

Delivery and Adoption

The third alternative is to deliver the baby and allow another couple to adopt him or her. You may feel that you are not capable of being a new parent at this time—and you may be giving a wonderful gift to a person or couple who is longing to love and raise a child. But this is an intense and the most personal of decisions, and it may have some emotional effects on you as you go through life. Again, the more help you can get from a counselor, the better.

Instant Replay

Sally, age 17, was not going to the senior dance in the spring because she couldn't get a baby sitter. She had thought that her boyfriend would eventually marry her once he saw the baby. But he had other things on his mind, and other plans to fulfill. And he just dropped out of the scene and left Sally alone to deal with their child.

Facing the Emotional Consequences of Sexual Activity

Knowing the score in the game of dating means being prepared for risks. It includes the risks of both physical and emotional relationships. Relationships are about people who care about each other; when something happens in those relationships to change them, such as beginning a sexual relationship, you both have to learn to adapt.

Getting too close too fast and for too long may also deprive you of the experience of dating many people. You begin to get a sense of what makes you happy, and what to look for in the people you date, by dating widely. However, if you become settled in an exclusive partnership too early, you may deny yourself the exciting possibility of sampling all that life has to offer.

Lessons Learned

Assessing whether you are ready for the big time and bright lights of relationships—dating, being together, and sex—is a powerful way to learn about yourself and others. Your life as a teenager is a wonderful series of adventures—and some misadventures. At times, looking at your life from the inside may not seem the most exciting, but these years will offer so many grand things for you to sample.

The dating game is the most fulfilling way to learn how to develop lasting relationships and to learn about yourself. You may see your dating game evolve into a serious match, and, eventually, you'll enter the finals of love and sex and their consequences. The good news is that with each game you play, as long as you play it with honesty and integrity, the better you become at it. Through your experiences, you'll strengthen your own personality while you learn how to develop healthy, happy relationships for today and in the future.

Instant Replay

Alec and Rachel were still together at age 20, after dating steadily since they were 15. As a matter of fact, they had never dated anyone else. And now, five years later and into a very serious relationship, they were having some problems. But they did not have the experience of having dated any other people. Alec wondered what life would be like with another girl; Rachel wondered if all guys were like Alec. In order to figure out whether the grass could be greener, they needed to go through the trauma of breaking up and seeing others. They had not had the opportunity of dating other people and seeing what other relationships were like. If they had, they might have been able to find greater satisfaction in their own backyard.

The Least You Need to Know

✧ If you decide to have sex, always use condoms.

✧ If you decide to have sex or engage in sexual activity, think about it in advance.

✧ There are physical and emotional consequences to having sex.

✧ The whole spectrum of the dating game provides opportunities to learn about yourself and to learn how to develop healthy relationships.

Bibliography

Bettelheim, Bruno. *Dialogues with Mothers*. New York: Avon Books, 1982.

Blackstone, Margaret, and Guest, Elissa. *Girl Stuff*. New York: Gulliver Books/Harcourt, Inc., 2000.

Boston Women's Health Collective. *The New Our Bodies, Our Selves*. New York: Touchstone Books/Simon & Schuster, 1992.

Canfield, Jack, Mark Victor Hansen, and Kimberly Kirberger. *Chicken Soup for the Teenage Soul III*. Deerfield Beach, Florida: Health Communications, Inc., 2000.

Chodorow, Nancy. *The Reproduction of Mothering*. Berkeley: University of California Press, 1978.

Coles, Robert. *The Moral Intelligence of Children*. New York: Plume Books/Random House, 1997.

Cook, Barbara. *How to Raise Good Kids*. Minneapolis: Bethany House Publishers, 1978.

Elium, Don, and Jeanne Elium. *Raising a Son*. Hillsboro, Oregon: Beyond Words Publishing, 1992.

———. *Raising a Teenager*. Berkeley: Celestial Arts, 1999.

Erikson, Erik. *Identity and the Lifecycle*. New York: W. W. Norton and Company, 1980.

Gianetti, Charlene, and Margaret Sagarese. *Parenting 911*. New York: Broadway Books, 1999.

Ginott, Haim. *Between Parent and Teenager*. New York: Avon Books, 1969.

Kirberger, Kimberly. *On Relationships*. Deerfield Beach, Florida: Health Communications, Inc., 1999.

McMahon, Tom. *Teen Tips*. New York: Pocket Books, 1996.

Ponton, Lynn. *The Sex Lives of Teenagers*. New York: Dutton Books/Penguin Group, 2000.

Rice, F. Phillip. *Intimate Relationships, Marriages, and Families*. Mountain View, California: Mayfield Publishing, 1999.

Riera, Michael. *Surviving High School*. Berkeley: Celestial Arts Publishing, 1997.

Sandoz, Bobbie. *Parachutes for Parents*. Lincolnwood, Illinois: Contemporary Books, 1997.

Sundberg, Janet, and Jim Sundberg. *Sports Parenting*. Colorado Springs: Waterbrook Press, 1984.

Trujillo, Michelle. *Why Can't We Talk?* Deerfield Beach, Florida: Health Communications, Inc., 2000.

Index

Symbols

84 Charing Cross Road, 31

A

abortion, 250
accepting dates, 69-70
Acquired Immune
  Deficiency Syndrome. *See*
  AIDS (Acquired Immune
  Deficiency Syndrome)
adaptability, making decisions, 179
adoption, 251
adulthood, planning for, 7
advice, asking for, 23
agreements, decisions, 179
AIDS (Acquired Immune
  Deficiency Syndrome),
  248-251
anger, dealing with, 162-165
anxieties, handling, 167-168
arguments
  handling, 116-117
  resolving, 164
Aspects of Love, 208
attraction
  reasons for, 60-61
  signs of, recognizing,
  103-104

automobiles, 10
  traffic laws, learning,
  188-190

B

Bettelheim, Bruno, 255
Between Parent and Teenager,
  256
birth control, 244-247
  coitus interruptus, 248
  contraceptive implants,
  247
  contraceptive jellies, 247
  contraceptive pills, 247
  diaphragms, 247
  methods, 246
  rhythm method, 248
Blackstone, Margaret, 255
breaking up, 120-126
  being dumped, 126-127
  danger signs, 122-124
  dealing with, 39
  dumping, 127
  fear of, 166
  learning from, 129

E

R